tobago

clean, green and serene

edited by Arif Ali

HANSIB

First published in Great Britain in 2005
Hansib Publications Limited
PO Box 226, Hertford SG14 3WY, England
Email: info@hansib-books.com
Website: www.hansib-books.com

ISBN 1 870518 97 7

Design and production by Graphic Resolutions, Hertfordshire, England

Printed and bound by Butler & Tanner, Somerset, England

Contents

Acknowledgments

The editor, Arif Ali, with Kenisha Thom, Trinidad and Tobago Miss World 2004 contestant, in discussion during the preparation of this book at Le Grand Courlan Resort, Black Rock, Tobago

FOLLOWING the publication, in 2000, of *Trinidad and Tobago: Terrific and Tranquil*, it was felt that a separate publication for Tobago was required to accompany the original title.

It is with great pleasure that we present *Tobago - Clean, Green and Serene.*

This publication would not have been possible without the help and support of many individuals and organisations.

We would like to thank Councillor Neil Wilson and the Tobago House of Assembly for commissioning the book; Joan Applewhite who encouraged us in the early stages and Carol Alfred and her team who were instrumental in getting the project off the ground. We are grateful to Sherma McDougall and Avion Hercules for their support and to Sumant Singh and the entire Tourism Department in Tobago. We thank the photographers and writers for their contributions and we are grateful to Rene Seepersadsingh, Nalini Galbarsingh and all the staff at Le Grand Courlan, Grafton Beach Resort and Singh's Auto Rentals for their support. Thanks also to Shareef Ali of Graphic Resolutions, who designed and managed the production of the book; Isha Persaud, for her persistence in sourcing information we required; Clement Williams, our main photographer; Simon Lee; Wayne Lee-Sing; Tanya Clovis; Sandie Hendrix; Dextor Trim; Lois Solomon; Richard Painter of Print Resources; Kash Ali of Books of Colour; Ella Barnes; Alan Cross; John Arnold; Stephen Broadbridge; Justin Joseph; Vernella Pilgrim; John Cooper; Jim Stephens; Christine Taylor; Janelle Aquing; Jessica Bensley; the translators, UPS; Charles Scott; Blue Waters Inn; the many others who offered support and information and Pamela Mary for your love and much care.

Arif Ali
September 2005

Hansib Publications is grateful to the following individuals, businesses and organisations for their support with this publication:

ANSA Mc AL Ltd
PO Box 100, 10/11 Floor
Tatil Building, 11 Maraval Road
Port of Spain
Tel: 625 3670/5, Fax: 624 8753

Arnos Vale Hotel
Arnos Vale Waterwheel Restaurant
AJM Tours, Arnos Vale Car Rentals
Franklyn Road, Plymouth
Tel: 639 2881, Fax: 639 4629
Email: manager@arnosvalehotel.com

Blue Horizon Resort
Jacamar Drive
Old Grange Road, Mt Irvine
Tel: 639 0433, Fax: 639 0432
www.blue-horizonresort.com

Chief Secretary's Office
Protocol Unit
Administrative Complex
Calder Hall
Tel: 639 2188, Fax: 639 5374
Email: thaprotocol@hotmail.com

Conrado Beach Resort Ltd
PO Box 405, Scarborough
Tel: 639 0145/6, Fax: 639 0755
Email: conrado@tstt.net.tt

Secretary of Tourism, Transport, Enterprise Development and Settlements
197 Doretta's Court, Mount Marie
Tel: 639 5126, Fax: 639 4369

Footprints Eco Resort
Culloden Bay
Tel: 660 0118, Fax: 660 0027
Email: footprints@trinidad.net

Grafton Beach Resort
Stonehaven Bay, Black Rock
Tel: 639 0191, Fax: 639 0030
Email: grafton@singhs.com

Hilton Tobago
PO Box 633, Scarborough
Tel: 660 8500, Fax: 660 8731
Email: tobhilt@tstt.net.tt

KAGM'S
PO Box 63, Grafton Beach Resort
Black Rock
Tel: 639 0191 ext 42
Fax: 639 6436

Kariwak Village Hotel
Crown Point
Tel: 639 8442, Fax: 639 8441
Email: kariwak@tstt.net.tt

Le Grand Courlan Spa Resort
Stonehaven Bay, Black Rock
Tel: 639 9667, Fax: 639 9292
Email: legrand@singhs.com

Republic Bank Ltd
PO Box 218
Commercial Business Centre
Scarborough
Tel: 639 2561, Fax: 639 3474
Email: email@republictt.com

TIDCO
Level 1 Maritime Center,
Barataria, Trinidad.
Tel: 675 7034, Fax: 638 3560
Email: tourism-info@tidco.tt

Tourism Development Company (TDS)
Dynacool Building, Tagarete Road
Port of Spain
Tel: 628 9427, Fax: 622 9415

Ministry of Tourism
51-55 Frederick Street
Port of Spain
Tel: 624 1403/623 8507
Fax: 625 0437/1825

Villa Being
50 Richmond Street, Port of Spain
Tel: 625 4443, Fax: 625 4420
Email: futures@tstt.net.tt

The International dialling code for Trinidad and Tobago is 868

Message

from Honourable Councillor Neil Wilson

Secretary of Tourism, Transportation,
Enterprise Development and Settlements
of the Tobago House of Assembly

Hon Neil Wilson / Come, discover
Tobago, the Capital of Paradise

A S Secretary for Tourism in the Tobago House of Assembly, I invite you to visit Tobago, the Capital of Paradise, where a warm and friendly people offer just the right level of hospitality to make vacationing a pleasurable experience.

Indeed Tobago's natural physical attributes and the methods that we employ to preserve them, have attracted worldwide attention and acclaim. Tobago is home to the oldest rainforest in the western hemisphere, a nature reserve that covers 10,000 acres of natural untouched vegetation, protected by law since 1776. This eco-system won Tobago the World Travel Awards prize for 'The Best Eco-Destination in the World' in 2003 and again in 2004.

Getting to us is easy. Daily and weekly flights are accessible from the United Kingdom through British Airways, Excel and Virgin Atlantic. If you are travelling from Continental Europe, Lauda Air will bring you out of Vienna, Martinair from Amsterdam and Condor from Frankfurt. As you set foot on Tobago, you will affirm that Tobago is indeed 'The Capital of Paradise'.

While you are in Tobago, take advantage of the domestic air route between Trinidad and Tobago and experience the diversity of our Twin-Island State. Fly via carriers LIAT, BWIA West Indies Airlines and Caribbean Star or travel by sea to exciting Trinidad aboard our inter-island fast-ferry service. Those who prefer a more laid back adventure may cruise into Port of Spain, our national capital, in a cozy cabin aboard our more luxurious liners.

Tobago continues to upgrade its Tourism product. Although we are acclaimed internationally for our leisure and Eco-Tourism, we continue to expand and diversify our product to include Sport, Academic, Cultural, Conference, and Health Tourism.

Live the leisure and sporting activities of your dreams. Dive into the tranquil waters of our marine paradise. Snorkel among Tobago's awesome coral reefs and rub shoulders with manta rays and myriad other marine life. Engage in documentary film-making, deep-sea diving, big game fishing, surfing, water-skiing and swimming or simply lie in the sun on the glistening sand. Imbibe the ozone, let the salty spray splash over your face as you skim the surface of the beautiful blue Caribbean sea in skiff or speed-boat, kayak or water scooter. Stroll barefooted on silver sand beaches in the moonlight and count the stars of the Milky Way or watch a thousand year old turtle weep upon the sand as she deposits her eggs.

Take a hike through our nature trails and see our spectacular array of butterflies and birds, the mysteries of our wetlands and our amazing flora and fauna. Browse our many historical forts and embattlements and discover the relics of our colonial past. Crest upon some quiet hill and hear the ominous sound of silence as you gaze into the timeless horizon.

Come and experience tranquil idyllic Crusoe's isle, this clean, green and serene wonderland, a destination of matchless tranquility, yet one that offers the heights of excitement. Abandon your cares and revel with us at our many feasts, fetes and festivals. Sample our culinary delights and dance to the pulsating rhythms of Calypso, Chutney and Soca music. We guarantee you an experience that will excite the spectrum of visitors, from the leisure seeker to the consummate academic.

Come, discover Tobago, the Capital of Paradise.

The National Flag

The national flag of Trinidad and Tobago was first used in 1962 when the nation gained its independence. Designed by the late George Bailey, it is made up of a black stripe bordered in white on a red background, each colour representing an element in the character of its land and people.

RED represents the vitality of the land, the warmth and energy of the sun and the courage and friendliness of its people.

WHITE represents the sea which surrounds the land, the cradle of its heritage, the purity of its aspirations and the equality of its people under the sun.

BLACK represents the dedication of the people joined together by one strong bond. It is the colour of strength, of unity, of purpose and of the wealth of the land.

The colours were chosen to represent the elements Earth, Fire and Water and to encompass the nation's past, present and future and to inspire it as one united, vital, free and dedicated people.

The Coat of Arms

The Coat of Arms was designed by the late George Bailey and was first used following independence in 1962. They show at the top a coconut palm in fruit and a ship's wheel representing the nation's colonial past. The national birds of the country - the Scarlet Ibis (found in Trinidad) and the Cocrico (found only in Tobago) - hold up the shield on which two Hummingbirds, another national bird, are depicted. Also on the shield are three Spanish galleons, the principal motifs of Trinidad and Tobago's British colonial seals. They all stand on three hills which represent the Trinity. The national watchwords, "Together We Aspire, Together We Achieve" form the base on which the insignia stands.

The National Flower

Tobago shares its national flower, the Chaconia (*Warszewiczia Coccinea*), with its sister island Trinidad. Also known as the 'Pride of Trinidad and Tobago' or a 'Wild Poinsettia', the Chaconia was named in honour of the last Spanish Governor of Trinidad, Don Jose Maria Chacon (1784-1797). This wild, forest flower is indigenous to the island and has long sprays of magnificent vermillion that are said to bloom around the anniversary of Trinidad and Tobago's Independence Day (August 31).

The National Seal

The National Seal dates back to 1815 and the words *Pulchrior evenit*, "She emerges more beautiful", represent Tobago's development nearly two hundred years later. Officially known as the 'Great Seal and Seal at Arms' it is used as the seal of the Tobago House of Assembly, the local governing administration. The current seal is a revised modern version of its ancestor, showing four ships sailing in the island's open harbour, a fruit laden coconut tree waving in the breeze and the sun rising over a hill. It is displayed in all government offices and on all official flags and documents.

The National Bird

Tobago's national bird is the Cocrico *(Ortalis ruficauda)* or Rufous-vented Chachalaca. Known locally as a Tobago Pheasant, it can be heard sounding a loud, grating chorus at dawn and dusk. It stands approximately 55cm *(22 inches)* tall and mainly inhabits the higher areas amidst the forest feeding on berries and small fruits.

Stephen Broadbridge

The National Pledge

"I solemnly pledge to dedicate my life
To the service of my God
And to my country.

I will honour my parents,
My teachers, my leaders and my elders,
And those in authority.

I will be clean and honest in all my thoughts,
My words and my deeds

I will strive, in everything I do
To work together with my fellowmen
Of every creed and race
For the greater happiness of all
And the honour and glory
Of my country."

Written by Marjorie Padmore

The National Anthem

Forged from the love of liberty
in the fires of hope and prayer
with boundless faith in our destiny
We solemnly declare

Side by side we stand
Islands of the blue Caribbean Sea
This our native land
we pledge our lives to thee

Here every creed and race
find an equal place
And may God bless our nation

Here every creed and race
find an equal place
And may God bless our nation.

Written by Patrick S. Castagne

Tobago Facts
at a Glance

50 miles (80 km)

TOBAGO

TRINIDAD

VENEZUELA

Official Name / Republic of Trinidad and Tobago

Capital / Scarborough

Location / Second most southerly of the Winward Islands of the Caribbean

Climate / Tropical Marine

Area / 300 sq. km (116 sq. miles)

Time Zone / GMT minus 4 hours

Major Ethnic Groups / African, East Indian, Mixed

Government Type / Parliamentary Democracy

Date of Independence / 31 August 1962

ISO Code / TT

Currency / Trinidad and Tobago Dollar TTD

Marble Island

London Bridge
Rock

**St. Giles and Melville
Islands**

North Point

Sisters Rocks

Corvo Point

Brothers Rocks

Charlotteville

**Police
Stn**

Flagstaff Hill

Hermitage

Man O' War
Bay

Belmont

Starwood

Cambleton

Black Rock

Bloody Bay

• L'Anse Fourmi

Fort Cambleton

Batteaux Bay

Parlatuvier Bay

Bloody Bay River

Speyside

Goat Island

• Parlatuvier

Northside Road

Gilpin Trail

Pigeon Peak
576m

*Trois
Rivieres*

**Little Tobago or
Bird of Paradise Island**

Parrot Hall

Roxborough Parlatuvier Road

Cape Gracias-a-dios

Main Ridge

Argyle River

Louis D'or River

Delaford

Merchiston

Tobago Forest Reserve

Belle River

Pedro Point

Argyle
Waterfall
W

**King's
Bay**

Great River

Morne D'or

Kendal Place

Louis D'or
**Police
Stn**

The Lure

Twin Rivers
Waterfall
W

Roxborough
Decompression
Chambor

Belle
Garden

Hillsborough
Dam

W

Rainbow
Waterfall

Richmond

**Police
Stn**

Carapuse Bay

Queen's Island

Pembroke •

• Glamorgan

Richmond Island

Windsor

Goodwood •

Goldsborough
Bay

Montrose

*Studley
Park*

Fort Granby

Ganby Point

Smith's Island

Symbol	Description	Symbol	Description	Symbol	Description
Highway		Lake / Pond			Beach
Road - main		★ Sightseeing			Dive Site
Road - secondary		Waterfall			Wreck
Under construction		Hiking			Reserve
Track		View Point			Bus Stop
One Way		P Parking			Petrol Leaded .. Unleaded
Runway		Fort			Post Office
River		Snorkeling			Traffic Lights

Map courtesy of Skyviews

Tobago - Clean, Green and Serene

top / life's a beach in Tobago

above & opposite / rainforest green

THE CIGAR-SHAPED island which the Amerindians named after the leaf they loved to smoke and which so dazzled Columbus he called it 'Bellaforma', lies 21 miles north-east of its sister island, Trinidad.

The 21-mile long and seven-mile wide tranquil Tobago, is surrounded by coral reefs. The low-lying coralline south west plateau rises gradually to a central ridge of volcanic hills reaching 1,890 ft. Throughout the eastern half, the white sand beaches, secluded bays and inlets of the Leeward or Caribbean coast and the rocky shoreline of the Windward Atlantic give way to dense rainforest (the oldest protected forest in the western hemisphere) covering the highlands, which are crossed by river valleys and waterfalls running south.

Until recent geological times, Tobago was part of the South American mainland. Consequently, it has an abundance of both mainland and island flora and fauna which is out of proportion to its size: 210 species of bird, 123 butterfly species, 24 types of snake (all harmless), 17 species of bat, 16 species of lizard, 14 species of frog and 12 types of mammal (including armadillo, agouti, opossum and peccary).

Originally inhabited by Amerindians, Tobago became a much-swapped pawn on the European colonial chessboard. Colonists from what is now Latvia, who settled in 1642, were the first to arrive. They were driven out by the Dutch in 1658, who were followed by successive waves of French and English invasions until the island was ceded to Britain by the 1802 Treaty of Paris. Tobago became a British Crown Colony in 1877 and following the collapse of the sugar industry, was joined with Trinidad as a political unit in 1888.

top / aerial view of Buccoo Reef

above / daily catch fresh from the sea

The majority of the 55,000 strong population are descendants of African slaves transported to work sugar, cotton and indigo plantations from the late 17th century onwards. In recent years, local Trinidadians (mainly vendors, storekeepers, hospitality workers and business people of East Indian origin - descendants of indentured labourers) and expatriates, drawn to the laid-back lifestyle, have added a new dimension to the population.

Culturally, however, Tobago's roots are strictly African Caribbean, unlike Trinidad's cosmopolitan diversity. African folklore and beliefs still flourish in the shade of silk cotton trees in hillside communities and the 'tambrin' drum of folk music plays to an African beat. Some of the best African traditions are showcased in their authentic village settings during the annual Heritage Festival in July but at any time of the year you are likely to stumble across a wake, harvest festival or a 'reel' dance dedicated to the ancestors.

With heavy industry restricted to Trinidad, Tobago remains largely unspoiled. Many islanders make their living from fishing or gardening (subsistence farming) but increasing numbers are now working in tourism, marketing the island's most valuable assets - its stunning natural resources.

Tobago is the south-east Caribbean's premier dive location. Below the waterline gently sloping pristine coral reefs, plunging submarine cliffs and volcanic formations offer exhilarating dives for both novices and advanced divers. Its serendipitous position, where the outflow of the Orinoco River, the Atlantic Ocean and Caribbean Sea meet, results in nutrient-rich waters teeming with life: nearly 300 species of hard coral; a wide variety of sponges; myriad tropical fishes and larger marine creatures including whales, sharks, dolphins, rare manta rays, squid and turtles.

While Scarborough is the island's national capital, the little fishing village of Speyside has become the dive capital, with its diversity of sites and the vortex of tidal streams around the offshore islands which make for superb drift dives. Although only established in the 1980s, the dive industry is operated professionally to international safety standards and Scarborough has a free decompression chamber facility.

On the waterline every conceivable water sport - from Hobie-Cat sailing to kite surfing and game fishing - is catered for; and those who prefer a more leisurely approach will appreciate reef spotting through glass-bottomed boats.

Back on land, Tobago has long been an attraction for ornithologists, naturalists and eco-tourists (including the internationally-acclaimed broadcaster David Attenborough, who filmed part of his 1990 television series *The Trials of Life* on Tobago) eager to sight the emblematic cocrico, hike through the Forest Reserve, scale waterfalls or watch turtles nesting on the beach at night. Mountain biking is an excellent and energising alternative to touring by car.

After an exquisite tropical sunset visitors will find a surprisingly full nightlife, which often showcases local culture. The weekly Sunday School beach party at Buccoo has become an institution for locals and visitors, as have the unique Easter goat and crab races and Tobago's own carnival - 'Tobago Fest'.

The economy is driven by tourism and real estate, with energy now being considered as a serious diversification possibility. Real estate development is actively encouraged and investment incentives, like exemption from customs duties on imported building materials and tourism-related equipment, have contributed to the many new developments on the island, including large hotel complexes, villa developments and two new shopping malls.

Visitors looking to invest in Tobago benefit not only from these exemptions but the real estate quota, which allows them to own up to five acres of land for commercial purposes, even without resident status. In terms of workforce development, the Tobago campus of the Trinidad and Tobago Hospitality and Tourism Training Institute provides training in craft, cuisine, hotel and tour operations and tourism management.

Just spend some time here and discover why the islanders say, "Tobago sweet."

top / watersport facilities at Le Grand Courlan Spa Resort

middle / a green turtle returns to sea after nesting on one of Tobago's many sandy beaches

above / local and international cuisine served with a smile

overleaf / Castara Bay on the leeward coast

top & middle / the business district around Scarborough

above / a local post box

Conducting Business in Paradise

TOBAGO with its emergence as a prime eco-destination platform seeks to improve its bid to become the headquarters of the Free Trade Areas of the Americas (FTAA). As Trinidad and Tobago vies to establish itself as the headquarters for the FTAA, the role of Tobago cannot be overlooked. In contrast to the energised, fast-paced and highly-industrialised environment that greets one in Trinidad, the sister isle has a spirit all of its own. Its capacity to entertain, mesmerize and challenge is ever present. Lying just off the northeastern end of Trinidad, it is the ideal destination to conduct business in paradise. Air carriers cruise the skies connecting Tobago with the rest of the Caribbean via LIAT and Caribbean Star and daily with the rest of the world.

Tobago is the second most southerly island in the Caribbean and with its multi terrain and variety of flora and fauna, its outstanding array of bird species and scores of brilliantly-hued butterflies, turquoise bays and distinct culture; the island has something to offer every visitor. It is no secret therefore that tourism has been, and continues to be, the mainstay of the island's economy. From the serious athlete to the fun adventurer, challenges are ever present. The sporting niche also includes scuba diving, game fishing, water sports, golf and cycling.

Tobago is home to the oldest protected rainforest in the western hemisphere. In October 2003, the World Travel Awards selected the Main Ridge Rainforest Reserve as the World's number one 'Eco-Tourism' destination. The scenery is ever changing and several of Tobago's waterfalls are also located here.

Tobago boasts several premier conference centres all strategically located. The

Clement Williams

Mt Irvine Bay Hotel, Hilton Tobago and Grafton Beach Resort are among those renowned for excellent conference facilities and customer service.

The Tobago House of Assembly is aggressively embarking on the development of core business and industrial parks with a view towards the diversification of the island's economic base through export based activities/industries. It is further envisaged that their bilateral arrangements will help promote Tobago as an investment platform both for tourism and for light industrial activities. In-house training and the outsourcing of certain aspects of development work are serving to empower and prepare the people of Tobago for FTAA. The close and meaningful working relationship between the public and private sector as is integral to Tobago's aim of presenting the perfect complement to Trinidad.

The island of Tobago is as unique and engaging as its people and culture. Besides a wide selection of land and water activities it offers unparalleled opportunities to invest and do business in a clean, green and serene environment.

Stephen Broadbridge

Stephen Broadbridge

top / gateway to the world - Crown Point International Airport

middle / a local tradeswoman minds her shop in Charlotteville

above / arriving at the Port

overleaf / downtown in Tobago's capital, Scarborough

Clement Williams

opposite top / the Esplanade

opposite bottom / dusk approaches
and the lights go on

above / a typical local Post Office

Clement Williams

opposite top / the Port

opposite bottom / Mason Hall

above / Scarborough seen from the air

Clement Williams

Clement Williams

Clement Williams

opposite top / President House better known as Governor's House. It was completed in1828 by the then Governor Major General Blackwell who was the first occupant. It is only occupied now when the President comes to Tobago

opposite bottom / the Republic Bank building in Scarborough

above / The village of Charlotteville, at one the end of Man O' War Bay, was named by the French. It has good bird watching with an abundance of wild parrots

overleaf / St Giles Island off the north east tip, home to many breeding bird colonies

Charles Scott

Clement Williams

top / Tobago's ferry port

above / the famous rustic jetty at Pigeon Point on Tobago's southern tip with its thatched beach huts and white sands is ideal for safe bathing all year round, as its waters are protected by nearby reefs

opposite top / BWIA operate flights to Trinidad, the Caribbean, north America and Europe

opposite bottom / a Virgin Atlantic arrival at Crown Point

Getting to and around Tobago

NATIONAL air carrier British West Indies Airways (BWIA) and Tobago Express, a subsidiary airline of BWIA, serve Tobago with daily nonstop return flights. Several other major airlines such as Excel Airways, British Airways, Virgin, Condor, Martinair, Lauda Air, all servicing the European routes while Caribbean Star and LIAT connect to the rest of the Caribbean. The national air carrier BWIA also flies to several North American destinations such as Miami, New York, Toronto and Washington DC via Trinidad. Visitors should check with the local Tourist Office for further information.

A ferry service shuttles daily between the islands of Trinidad and Tobago. The trip is approximately 4-5 hours and offers cabin accommodation and space for cargo and vehicles. A new fast ferry service has been added to the route. Maximum duration of each trip is two and a half hours.

A number of reputable car rental agencies offer motor vehicles at affordable prices. You will need an international driving licence or one that has been issued in either the USA or Europe. Remember to drive on the left side!

Island tours are available with many of the registered taxis. They display licence plates that begin with the letter 'H'. Alternatively, one of the best ways of seeing the island is by public transport. The Public Transportation Services Corporation (PTSC) can be contacted for bus schedules or the local tourist office will have this information. There are also buses that are known locally as 'maxi-taxis' operating certain routes on the island. These can be identified by the blue horizontal bands along the body and have an 'H' registration plate.

Clement Williams

Clement Williams

top / Tobago's tropical flora

middle / Mt Irvine golf course

above / Grafton Beach Resort - one of the larger of Tobago's hotels located at the southern end of the island

Tobago: The Capital of Paradise

GOOD THINGS they say, especially with reference to Tobago, come in small packages. Here tropical warmth mediated by cooling breezes sets the mood for pure relaxation and rejuvenation. The natural ambience of the isle mesmerises with white sand beaches and turquoise warm waters; dense rainforest and volcanic hills; picturesque fishing and hillside villages; a constant chorus of birdsong and tumbling waterfalls.

You could pick a different beach for every day of your stay, or once Tobago has eased body and soul, choose from an amazing range of activities: golfing on championship courses; riding with manta rays; betting on the goat races or helping pull in the fisherman's seine; horse riding on the shoreline or high in the hills; getting to know islanders at a harvest festival or jumping up with them for carnival. The choices are unlimited and yours.

Similarly when it comes to accommodation the choices are endless: a self-catering apartment a hop skip and jump from the beach; a holistic retreat with on-call masseur; lavish resorts and spas with their own watersports, tennis courts, conference and ballrooms; family-run guesthouses and dive lodges; eco and nature resorts, or luxury villas.

While most of the larger hotels and resorts, along with many smaller guesthouses and apartments are located at the southwest end of the island, with a high density at Crown Point within a few minutes' walking distance of the airport, it's now possible to pick one's spot and find suitable accommodation.

Stephen Broadbridge

Tobagonians love their food so you're never far from the best local or international cuisine and if you feel obliged to keep contact with the folks back home or some unfinished business Tobago has broadband, internet and cyber cafes. The lifestyle may be what islanders call back in times and the pace of life is as slow as you could wish it, but Tobago has all necessary links with the 21st century-as long as you want them.

Coco Reef Resort & Spa

Le Grand Courlan Resort

Blue Waters Inn

top / the beach at Pigeon Point

left / the pool at the Coco Reef Resort

middle & above / fine food and friendly service at Le Grand Courlan Resort and at the Blue Waters Inn

Blue Waters Inn

Stephen Broadbridge

above / the bay at Blue Waters Inn. The area surrounding this hotel has an abundance of birds and other wildlife. The hotel has its own tennis courts and dive school which utilises the 180-foot private dock (pictured). It offers snorkelling, kayaking, glass bottomed boat trips, rainforest tours, aromatherapy, massage and cosmetic treatments. Its reputation as 'the best kept secret on the island' is well deserved

left / the Nylon Pool at Buccoo Reef. Affectionately named so after Princess Anne, while on her honeymoon in 1973, is said to have commented that the waters were as clear as looking through nylon stockings. The waters are only two to three feet deep while over a mile from the shore

opposite / the cool waters and beach at the Blue Waters Inn

overleaf / the protected nature reserve of Buccoo Reef

Blue Waters Inn

Grafton Beach Resort

Villa Being

some of Tobago's luxury hotels / Grafton Beach Resort (above), Villa Being (left) and Le Grand Courlan (opposite)

overleaf top / the secluded cove of the Arnos Vale Hotel, nestled amidst the gentle slopes of a 450 acre tropical Estate teeming with exotic birds and other wildlife. The resort is rich in history with the Arnos Vale Estate dating back to its use as a sugar plantation and even further back to when the indigenous Carib Indians inhabited Tobago. The sandy beach is one of the finest the island offers and the bay is considered one of the best for snorkelling. The resort also has a state of the art dive centre catering for all abilities.

overleaf bottom / one of Tobago's many unspoilt beaches

Le Grand Courlan Resort

Arnos Vale Hotel

Tobago Tourism Authority

Grafton Beach Resort

Grafton Beach Resort

these pages / situated on the south west of Tobago overlooking the Caribbean Sea at beautiful Stone Haven Bay just five miles from the airport is the ever popular Grafton Beach Resort. Set amongst five acres with a backdrop of Tobago's lush tropical hills, the fully-inclusive Grafton Beach Resort provides a warm welcome and comfortable accommodation. With sports facilities including a dedicated dive centre, non-motorised watersports, Kids Klub, air-conditioned squash courts, wedding and games room, superb food and some of the best cocktails in the area.

Grafton Beach Resort

Grafton Beach Resort

Villa Being

opposite / palm trees in Tobago's tropical landscape

above / relaxing by the poolside at Villa Being at Arnos Vale on Tobago's leeward coast

Kariwak Village Hotel

opposite top / Footprints Eco Resort aims to preserve and protect the environment while maintaining the comfort of its guests. The buildings are designed to complement the beauty of the blue Caribbean waters and Tobago's green rolling hills. The wood used in the construction of the resort is all locally grown or native to the region. The roofs of some of the buildings are made from the leaves of the timit palm - an echo of the first material ever used for roofing in Trinidad and Tobago. The resort covers 61 acres and is a 35 minute drive from Crown Point airport. Guests are invited to become involved in the current conservation efforts by planting a tree during their stay. The resort has saltwater pools which draw water directly from Culloden Bay and a pristine reef in the bay offers excellent snorkelling.

opposite bottom / find yourself one of Tobago's beaches

this page / Kariwak Village, Tobago's charming, award-winning small hotel and restaurant. A short walk from the beach, Kariwak is an oasis in the lively Crown Point area, with an enviable reputation for its unassuming "hippy-chic" flair. It has carved a distinctive niche with its holistic approach to holidays that soothe the body, mind and the spirit. The hotel has intimate accommodation, exquisite food, revitalising massage treatments, lush tropical gardens dominated by the thatched roof ajoupa and it is a centre for tai chi, yoga and meditation. The restaurant, supplied with fresh herbs from its kitchen garden, serves delicious meals by friendly staff in an open air Caribbean setting. The Usha Holistic Health Center hosts some of the finest alternative health professionals on the island, offering a variety of body treatments that merge the ancient practices of touch and movement with the latest technologies of light and water to balance and rejuvenate the body's natural energy system.

Kariwak Village Hotel

Le Grand Courlan Resort

Le Grand Courlan Resort

Le Grand Courlan Resort

Le Grand Courlan Resort

these pages / Located on picturesque Stone Haven Bay, the fully-inclusive Le Grand Courlan Spa Resort provides luxury, elegance, comfort and convenience to make this one of Tobago's most idyllic retreats. It offers beachfront accommodation, an oversized swimming pool with swim-up bar, a fabulous blend of local and international cuisine in a choice of restaurants and daily spa treatments, dive centre, non-motorised watersports and many other activities. Two flood-lit tennis courts are among its many amenities. For those looking to rest, relax and feel pampered, this resort will offer something for couples, those wishing to marry or honeymooners alike.

Hilton Tobago Golf & Spa Resort

Hilton Tobago Golf & Spa Resort

previous page & these pages /
Located in the south-west of Tobago is
the Hilton Tobago Golf & Spa Resort.
Nestled in twenty acres of tropical
beachfront and only fifteen minutes
from Crown Point International
Airport, the three-story resort reflects
the plantation setting of its
surroundings. Overlooking its own 18-
hole PGA-designed championship golf
course, the ultra-modern style resort
offers amenities for the total comfort
of its guests including a gymnasium,
tennis courts, sauna, massage,
watersports and a children's club. Each
of the 200 ocean-front rooms has a
private balcony with views of the lush
gardens and sparkling waters of the
Atlantic. The resort has a wide choice
of cuisine at a number of restaurants.
There is an elegant seafood restaurant,
a more casual all-day diner and a lively
grill offering snacks and cocktails. At
the poolside is a relaxing swim-up bar.
Guests can also unwind in the lobby
lounge or enjoy live entertainment in
the main hotel bar. Making the most
of Tobago's world-renowned
snorkelling and scuba diving the resort
also operates a PADI dive school.

Hilton Tobago Golf & Spa Resort

Hilton Tobago Golf & Spa Resort

previous page / the sun sets over the lagoon at Lambeau, near Scarborough

above / Castara Bay

left / sunset over Crown Point, Tobago's most westerly point, the best place to see out the day

opposite / the end of another day at the Conrado Beach Resort - a small family-run hotel at Pigeon Point - an ideal location with an authentic Caribbean flavour

Conrado Beach Resort

Le Grand Courlan Resort

Saying "I do" in Tobago
Legal requirements and useful information

Charles Scott

THERE IS NO better island for two hearts to be joined than Tobago. This island of 'Old World' romance and charm is washed in with professional wedding planners to make the happiest day of your life become the most treasured one.

Prerequisites for a Special Marriage Licence

/ Both parties must be non-residents of Trinidad and Tobago

/ Both parties must be in the country of Trinidad and Tobago for a minimum of three days after the date of their arrival.

/ All non-English documents produced must be translated into English and be notarised.

/ Both parties must present proof of residence and identification in the form of passports and produce their airline tickets.

/ If divorced, the original or notarised copy of decree absolute must be produced.

/ If widowed, an original death certificate must be presented.

/ Persons under the age of 18 years must have written consent from a parent or legal guardian.

/ A deed poll or other proof of name change, where name may differ on documents, must be presented

/ A marriage licence fee of TT $337.5 or US $50.00, which is payable by cash, is applicable.

Visitors are welcome to apply at any of the following offices

/ Registrar General's Office, Jerningham Street, Scarborough, Tobago Tel: 868 639-3210

/ The Board of Inland Revenue, Sangsters Hill, Scarborough, Tobago Tel: 868 639-2410

Other requirements to consider:

/ Visitors should note that a certified marriage officer in a public place may perform marriages on any given day between the hours of 6.00 am and 6.00 pm. Prior to the marriage ceremony, the licence must be presented to the officiating officer.

/ In Tobago, all marriages are considered civil except for Orisha, Hindu and Muslim ceremonies, which have additional requirements.

/ Most countries automatically recognise our marriages as legal. Others may require certain procedures to be carried out at member consulates or embassies in Trinidad or upon return to resident country. We advise that visitors check the requirements of their country with regard to overseas marriages.

Blue Waters Inn

Discover Tobago's Underwater Secrets

opposite / a coral reef off Tobago. Because of its vicinity to the rich food source of the Orinoco river, the seas around Tobago have some of the most diverse diving in the Caribbean. An array of different varieties of coral including the world's largest brain coral, fish including manta rays, varied plant life and other sea life including sea turtles and seahorses can be found - as can wrecks and dive walls. It is said that diving in Tobago is as unspoiled as the island

above / the dive school at the Blue Waters Inn

SCUBA DIVING is one of the fastest growing sports worldwide and Tobago is one of the best-kept secrets of the underwater world. Blessed with nutrient rich waters the marine life is diverse and abundant. Situated at the end of the Caribbean islands, Tobago offers a variety of dive sites unparalleled in the region for species diversity. At times the effluence from the Orinoco River in South America may adversely affect underwater visibility. However, it is these nutrients that provide sustenance to the reefs giving Tobago a wonderful variety of healthy coral and fish life.

Water temperatures range from "summertime" highs of 82°F *(28°C)* to lows of 75°F *(24°C)* in January and February. Most divers find that 3mm neoprene is sufficient thermal protection.

The currents vary in strength from site to site, so there is something for every experience level, from novice to the most experienced. Wreck diver, photographer, explorer, whatever your preference, see Caribbean scuba diving at its best.

The wreck of the *M/V Maverick* sits at 100ft *(33m)* and is waiting to be explored. Originally named *The Scarlet Ibis,* she was the first passenger ferry between Trinidad and Tobago. Before being sunk as a dive site in April 1997, she was cleaned, inspected and made safe for divers. Snappers and Rainbow Runners lurk in the shadows inside the car deck and schools of baitfish swirl across the upper deck at a depth of 60ft *(18m)*, making it accessible to all diver certification levels.

Arnos Vale is a shallow dive (maximum 40ft/*13m*) and as such, allows maximum bottom time for checking out the nooks and crannies, for lobsters, eels and the elusive Torpedo rays in the sand.

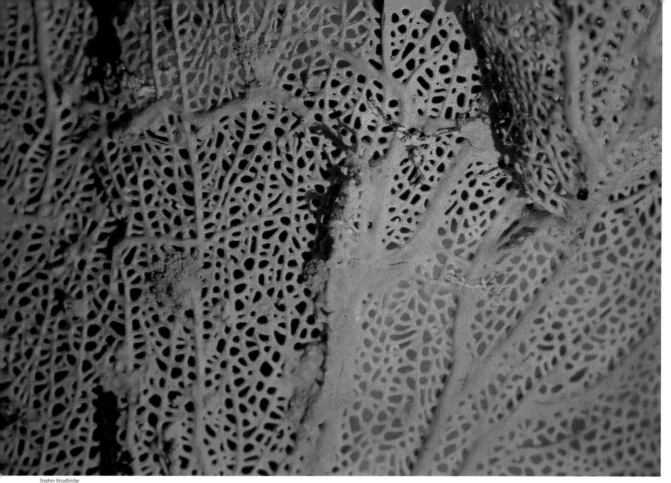

Stephen Broadbridge

At the northwestern end of the island, The Sisters is a series of rock pinnacles rising up from the deep. This is where you may see Hammerheads and Manta rays.

London Bridge is the most well-known and spectacular site around the St Giles Islands, off the island's northeastern tip. Tarpon, turtles and sharks are frequently sighted and a good eye can find octopus in the holes in the rock face. Another favourite area with divers is Boulder Valley at the mouth of Man-O-War Bay, where divers zigzag among the huge sponge and coral encrusted boulders.

Around the corner from St Giles, on the Atlantic side of the island, is Speyside. Most of the dives here are drift dives along the sloping reefs around the two offshore islands, Little Tobago and Goat Island. Kelleston Drain is home to what is reputed to be the largest brain coral in the Caribbean and according to some, in the world.

Japanese Gardens begins on a shallow slope covered with Vase sponges, purple Rope sponge and green algae growth. Thousands of bicolour Damselfish flit among the sponges looking like butterflies in a miniature Japanese Garden. A hard right turn between two large rocks and the current takes you through Kamikazee Cut, leading you into completely different terrain. Here the slope is much steeper and the reef is covered with brightly coloured sponges and corals. Seemingly unending soft coral growth sprouts from the granular white sand on the reef top.

The Association of Tobago Dive Operators, formed in 1996, has enabled dive operators to work together to maintain the highest standards of safety and enjoyment for the sport and provides up-to-date information on all aspects of diving in Tobago.

Stephen Broadbridge

opposite / diving off the beach at the Blue Waters Inn

top / close up of a sea fan coral

above / Goat Island

Stephen Broadbridge

top / a giant leatherback turtle laying her eggs on one of Tobago's beaches

above / a hatchling reaches the sea

Witness the Wonder of Nesting Sea Turtles

THERE ARE FEW more awe-inspiring sights than the giant leatherback's *(Dermochelys coriacea)* ancient egg-laying ritual. For 200 million years these gentle marine behemoths (the world's largest sea turtles at up to 500kg or1100 lbs) have dragged themselves up onto beaches in the tropic regions to excavate nests in beach sand and deposit their precious eggs.

The sight of a leatherback female crying as she lays (they secrete a fluid, "tears", to keep their eyes clear when they are out of the water) is an experience few forget. Perhaps they weep for the past. Giant leatherbacks are now a critically endangered species - a 1995 estimate of nesting female leatherbacks put their number at 34,500, down from 115,000 in 1980. And Tobago is one of the few places privileged to be a leatherback maternity home and hatchling nursery.

Between March and June every year, giant leatherback turtles visit some of Tobago's northern beaches to lay their eggs. Turtle hatchlings emerge between 55 and 70 days later, which itself is a wonder to behold.

Only a handful of turtles out of every 1000 hatchlings ever reach maturity. Female leatherbacks reach nesting age when they are about 25 years old, and only lay every two years. They require soft, dry sand to nest and the greatest density of nests is found on an expanse of beach between Turtle Beach Hotel and the Black Rock River. Green and hawksbill sea turtles also nest in Tobago, but the leatherback turtle is the most common species encountered. All three species are considered endangered.

Local conservation efforts include the group SOS Tobago (Save Our Sea Turtles).

Blue Waters Inn

SOS actively monitors Tobago's sea turtle populations and reports its findings to relevant governmental agencies and international organisations including the World Wildlife Foundation and Earth-watch.

above / a giant leatherback turtle off the shores of Batteaux Bay

In addition, Tobago, along with other Caribbean nations, is a part of the Wider Caribbean Sea Turtle Conservation Network (Widecast) project, which works toward the conservation of six species of endangered and critically endangered sea turtles found regionally. Tobago is also a signatory to international environmental agreements such as CITIES and The Cartagena Convention (Protection & Development of the Marine Environment of the Wider Caribbean Region).

Turtle Watching and Protection Guidelines:
- *When near or approaching turtles, be absolutely quiet*
- *Extinguish all lights, including video camera lights and camera flashes*
- *Observe a 50-feet (15-metre) exclusion zone around turtles until the nest is ready and laying begins*
- *Approach quietly and be careful not to disturb the nest in any way*
- *Never handle turtle eggs or attempt to ride turtles' backs*
- *A few photos may be taken only when the turtles are headed back to sea*
- *Help protect sea turtles by not selling or purchasing sea turtle products*
- *Don't throw rubbish into the sea and don't litter beaches*

Sea turtles play a very important role in the ocean's ecosystems. As part of marine fauna in Tobago's offering of eco-diversity, we are privileged to invite nature-lovers to enjoy the wondrous spectacle of our nesting sea turtles.

/ *Wayne Lee-Sing*

above / giant leatherback turtles nesting on Tobago's beaches

SOS Tobago's Turtles

SEA TURTLES have inhabited the world's oceans for millions of years and have been a traditional source of food in the Caribbean. Tobago's reefs and sea grass beds are blessed with small resident populations of Hawksbill and green sea turtles. From March to August they provide a temporary breeding and nesting refuge for the migratory giant Leatherbacks. Sea turtles have been hunted at sea and on land for centuries and are now endangered worldwide; with the Hawksbills and Leatherbacks being critically so. Poaching, pollution, coastal development and the commercial fishing industry have all taken their toll on the fragile sea turtle populations. Most sea turtles take up to 25 years to reach sexual maturity and in most cases, they are dying faster than they can reproduce.

Save Our Sea Turtles (SOS) Tobago was officially formed in February 2000, with a mission to conserve Tobago's turtles and their local marine and coastal habitats through community-based initiatives in research, education and ecotourism. In the beginning, this tiny action-oriented group focused exclusively on nesting-beach patrols in the Black Rock/Grafton area. However, the organization continues to develop with assistance from volunteers and donors; from government agencies like the Department of Tourism; and organisations like the UK-based Travel Foundation.

SOS Tobago's activities centre on the turtle-nesting season, which runs from March to August. The SOS volunteer beach patrol team is still the backbone of SOS Tobago's research and protection programme, focusing primarily on providing nightly coverage of three key Leatherback nesting beaches in the Black Rock area with smaller teams performing spot checks at other important nesting sites. SOS Beach Patrol works closely with the Department of Natural Resources and the Environment Wildlife Section to ensure the safety of nesting female sea turtles and to collect valuable research data on the local population.

Monitoring and enforcement can only do so much to reduce the traditional consumption of turtle meat and eggs. Education is by far the most viable, long-term conservation strategy. SOS Tobago conducts a comprehensive educational programme at schools throughout the island that incorporates turtle-watching field trips for students and their parents. Lectures are also held at village councils, libraries, churches and other community forums during the nesting season. Turtle issues are highlighted during this time via the media and online in an effort to raise public awareness and appreciation of turtle conservation.

The SOS ecotourism team takes the education programme a step further by seeking to demonstrate to the communities close to the beaches that a nesting turtle can be more economically valuable than a pot of turtle stew. Exploring the possibilities of turtle conservation with tour guides, hotels, communities and tourists has helped to encourage a great deal of local support, particularly in the Black Rock area. Groups of visiting university students have helped to

Stephen Broadbridge

supplement SOS Tobago's understaffed beach patrol team and have also filled small guest houses that would otherwise be empty in the quiet tourist months of May and June. Guided turtle-watching tours are becoming more popular to those looking for a once in a lifetime experience.

In response to crowd control issues on the busier beaches, turtle-watching guidelines have been developed in collaboration with the tour guides and the Department of Natural Resources. Tour groups are controlled in terms of size and distance from the turtles and flash photography is totally banned. Regular SOS training sessions for the tour guides and beachfront hotel staff provide opportunities to discuss the latest turtle information as well as to review the turtle watching guidelines.

In spite of its small achievements, SOS Tobago feels this is just the beginning. Every nesting season brings new ideas and exciting possibilities. The research, education and eco-tourism opportunities are endless. Sea turtles are the ultimate flagship species for Tobago and focusing on their preservation also brings into sharper focus the need to protect their nesting and feeding habitats and our beautiful beaches from the ravages of irresponsible human activities. Sea turtle conservation has grown considerably over the last few years in Tobago and its continuing evolution is certainly integral to the continuing evolution of our green, clean and serene Tobago.

| Tanya Clovis

top | a giant leatherback lays her eggs while turtle-watchers look on

middle | a green sea turtle nesting

above | a giant leatherback nests in the early morning

top / the Dwight Yorke Stadium

middle / superstar footballer Dwight Yorke pictured while playing for Manchester United

above / tennis facilities can be found at the Blue Waters Inn

Other Sport in Tobago

WHILE TOBAGO is justifiably regarded as one of the Caribbean's and indeed the world's premier dive locations, the island has much more to offer sport wise, on land and offshore. The Mt Irvine international golf course and the more recent Tobago Plantations course are among the most scenic greens in the region; horse riding along the shoreline and inland is gaining in popularity as is off-road mountain biking; both activities allowing riders access to off-the-beaten-track areas.

Thanks to superstar Dwight Yorke, football now vies with long established cricket as most popular local sport. Born in Canaan, Yorke began his career playing beach and village football, before captaining his school team Signal Hill, graduating to the national team for the 1989 World Cup and then being signed to Aston Villa, before transferring to Manchester United for the record fee of £12.6 million. After spells at Blackburn Rovers and Birmingham City, he signed for the Australian club Sydney FC in 2005. Both football and cricket are widely followed. The main grounds are the Dwight Yorke Stadium Bacolet, (home of island team Tobago United), Shaw Park, Signal Hill, Roxborough sporting complex and Plymouth. Other popular local sports are basketball, netball and volleyball and there are tennis courts at some hotels.

Game fishing attracts similar numbers as diving, as Tobago waters literally teem with fishlife. The offshore season, which runs from October through June, gives game fishermen the chance to catch deep sea species like white and blue Marlin, Sailfish, Tuna, Wahoo, Swordfish and Mako Shark, while coastal fishing

Clement Williams

offers Tarpon, Bonefish, Permit and Snook and even the reefs can be fished for King Mackerel, Barracuda, Snapper, Grouper and Jacks.

Watersports obviously feature prominently: there are several yachting regattas and between April and November Mt Irvine Bay is popular with surfers. The lagoon off Pigeon Point is ideal for windsurfing, kite and parasailing and other beaches offer Hobie Cat sailing, water and jet skiing and kayaking facilities.

Sporting calendar

January: Pro Am Golf, Mt Irvine

March: Tobago International Game Fish tournament-offshore qualifying event for Rolex/International Game Fish Association competition

April: Easter Tuesday Goat and Crab races, Buccoo.
Carib International Game Fishing Tournament, Pigeon Point

May: Angostura/Yachting World Regatta

June: 2005 inaugural Optimist North American Championship sailing competition for 10-15 year-olds

August: Great Race, annual powerboat classic, Store Bay.
Tobago Open Golf Tournament, Mt Irvine

October: Malta Carib International Cycle Classic

Clement Williams

top / the Malta Carib International Cycle Classic takes place in October

above / Tobago-born international cyclist Emile Abraham

Clement Williams

Tobago Tourism Authority

above / a near collision at the Angostura/Yachting World Regatta

left / playing a round of golf on one of Tobago's idyllic courses

opposite & overleaf / first class facilities at the Dwight Yorke Stadium

sporting variety / cricket on a local ground (above), tennis at the Blue Waters Hotel (left), Kayaking (below) and the Great Race, Tobago's annual powerboat classic (opposite)

Charles Scott

Charles Scott

Charles Scott

Blue Waters Inn

A Paradise for Birdwatchers

EVERYDAY is a lucky day for birdwatchers in Tobago! From tanagers to mockingbirds, humming-birds to woodpeckers, there's almost nowhere in this unspoilt, verdant isle that isn't a birdwatcher's paradise. Even built-up areas come alive, with vibrant motmots and hummingbirds enticing you from a verandah railing or a fire-red hibiscus. Such is Tobago's natural attraction to avifauna, over 210 species of birds have been spotted revelling in this natural paradise only 42 by 10 kilometres (26 by 7 miles). Few, if any, destinations can claim a higher density of bird varieties.

Tropical Tobago seems almost purposely designed to attract birds. Like its more developed partner Trinidad, Tobago was once attached to the South American mainland which accounts for the incredible diversity of fauna and flora. Together, Tobago and Trinidad have more bird species than the rest of the Caribbean combined.

The position of the islands - just 10 miles off the coast of Venezuela at the southernmost tip of the West Indian archipelago - also makes them an ideal stopover point for migratory birds. Many northern birds either stay in Tobago during winter or pass through on their way to southern wintering grounds. Conversely, during the sub-equatorial winter months, some southern species from as far as Argentina regularly visit Tobago. This diversity of bird species also relates directly to the island's varied habitats: including tropical rainforests, freshwater wetlands, mangrove swamps and fairly isolated coastal islands.

Some of the more well-known birdwatching sites in Tobago include the Main Ridge Forest Reserve, Little Tobago, St Giles Islands, Store Bay, Buccoo, Mount Irvine,

opposite / a blue-and-yellow macaw (*Ara ararauna*)

top / bananaquits (*Coereba flaveola*) known locally as a Sugareater or Sucrier. Its large population can be seen in most areas throughout Tobago

middle / Tobago's National Bird, the cocrico (*Ortalis ruficanda*) or Tobago Pheasant, a very common inhabitant frequenting hillsides and scrub

above / birdwatchers on the look out for Tobago's tropical fauna

Clement Williams

top / a blue crown motmot *(Momotus momota)* known locally as the King of the Woods. Seen in heavily shaded parts of the forest and on plantations

above / a palm tanager *(Thraupis palmarum)*

opposite / a red crown woodpecker *(Malenerpes rubricapillus)* and a blue grey tanager *(Thraupis episcopus)*

Plymouth, Hillsborough Dam, Grafton and Caledonia Bird and Wildlife Sanctuary, Adventure Farm & Nature Reserve and Cuffie River Nature Retreat. But anywhere in Tobago is a birdwatching site. Keep your eyes peeled and your binoculars or camera at the ready and intimate birdwatching treats might be in store.

Surrounded by Seabirds

Although replete with birds of every description, seabirds occupy a special place for Tobago birdwatchers. Two small islands off the coast of Tobago, Little Tobago and St Giles Island, are world renowned for the seabird colonies that inhabit them. Keep in mind that for conservation purposes landings are controlled and you may need a permit and guide.

Little Tobago is about a mile long and considered one of the most important seabird sanctuaries in the Caribbean. It is accessible only by boat from Speyside and is a trip well worth taking. Up to 58 species have been recorded on Little Tobago (not counting the Bird of Paradise or Water Fowl), 33 of them breeding. There are substantial colonies of Audubon shearwaters, bridled and Noddy terns, laughing gulls, brown boobies and breathtaking red-billed tropicbirds dancing along the cliffs with their amazing long, billowing tails. Well-marked trails lead to cliffside vantage points that leave you breathless. Hop on a glass-bottomed boat and enjoy Angel Reef on the way.

Little Tobago is also called Bird of Paradise Island because the eccentric bird lover, Sir William Ingram, introduced 24 pairs of Papua New Guinea's Greater Bird of Paradise there. The Birds of Paradise are no more. They never fared that

Clement Williams

Clement Williams

Anhinga (Anhinga anhinga) / the Snake Bird or Black Duck has a small population found mainly in inland waters, swamps, rivers or reservoirs like Hillsborough Dam

Duck (Anas bahamensis) / the Brown duck or Wild duck mainly frequents the swamp lands in south western Tobago where they breed. A protected Game bird hunted in the open season

Egret (Bubulcus ibis) / the Cowbird or Tickbird is a very common resident of Tobago. Seen in savannahs and marshes as well as dumping grounds. It roosts in or around swamp lands

Frigate bird (Fregata magnificens) / known locally as the Scissorstail, Weatherbird or Man 'O'War. Common in many coastal areas of Tobago with breeding colonies on St Giles Island. Although fully protected it suffers from some poaching

Gallinule (Gallinula chloropus) / the Waterhen or Moorhen is a common species in swamps and marshes and waterways

Green parrot (Amazona amazonica) / a very common species found especially in hill forests and cultivated areas

Heron (Florida caerulea) / the Blue Gaulding. is a fairly common species which inhabits swamps, flooded fields, marshes and sea coasts throughout the island

Ibis (Eudocimus ruber) / the Scarlet Ibis is known locally as a Flamingo. Not common in Tobago but some have been seen in mangrove swamps and wetlands on its south-western side - probably strays from Trinidadian flocks. It is fully protected and is Trinidad's National Bird

Jacamar (Galbula ruficanda) / known as a King Hummingbird this is a fairly common resident on roadsides in the forest and old cocoa plantations

Kingfisher (Chloroceryle americana) / the Fisherman is a common resident which frequents forest streams and swamps

Noddy (Anous stolidus) / known locally as a Brown Noddy. Common offshore and on breeding islands of Little Tobago and St Giles

Clement Williams

Clement Williams

top / a hummingbird

above / a red billed tropic bird *(Phaethon aethereus)* nesting with its chick. Known locally as a Boasten, this common oceanic species often frequents the islets off Tobago, especially Little Tobago and St Giles

opposite / a southern lapwing *(Vanellus chilensis)* is a migratory bird frequenting marshy savannahs and open areas usually near water and is often seen in pairs

Clement Williams

Oropendola (Psarocoius decumanus) / known locally as the Yellowtail or Corn Bird. A common species which frequents forests and cultivated areas with large trees. Also occurs on Little Tobago and St Giles Island. Regarded largely as an agricultural pest

Pelican (Pelicanus occidentalis) / known locally as a Big Ben. Common on all coasts of Tobago mostly in flocks which vary in size from place to place

Quail dove (Geotrygon linearis) / known locally as the Mountain Dove. This species occurs mostly in south-western areas of Tobago and at higher levls in the forest

Silverbeak (Sporophila nigricollis) / a very uncommon species whose population have been affected by excessive trapping and habitat destruction. Although protected, it is threatened with extinction

Spinetail (Synallaxis cinnamornea) / a common species found in hill forests and scrubland

Trogon (Trogon collaris) / the Red-Bellied Trogon is uncommon in forest and scrubland. Although protected, its numbers have yet to recover from the effects of Hurricane Flora in 1963.

Vireo (Vireo olivaceus) / known locally as the Caribbean Vireo. An uncommon and protected species found in lowland forests, cocoa plantations and gardens.

Whimbrel (Numenius phaepus) / known locally as a Crooked-Bill. Frequents the swamps and mudflats, mainly in the south-west

Yellowlegs (Tringa flavipes) / are a fully protected migratory species which frequents swamps, mudflats and flooded pastures. Fairly common throughout the year with numbers highest from August to November.

Zenaida dove (Zenaida auriculata) / the Wood Dove is a recent arrival to the island and is now fairly common

well outside of their native environment and Hurricane Flora in 1963 put paid to the few that remained. But Little Tobago's native species more than make up for a spectacular bird-watching experience.

St Giles Island, at 72 acres the largest of the group, supports one of the region's most important large seabird breeding colonies. Magnificent frigatebirds, the red-footed booby, red-billed tropicbirds, Audubon's shearwater, Noddy terns and brown boobies all have been sighted, with reports of many other species. Twenty four types of land birds also have been recorded. Accessibility to St Giles is not as easy as Little Tobago.

So come to Tobago for a bird's eye view. Our birds, and our beauteous island, are calling.

/ Wayne Lee-Sing

Tobago Tourism Authority

Tobago Tourism Authority

above / the diversity of Tobago's flora is largely due to its variable topography. A main ridge runs down from the northern end of Tobago for nearly two thirds of its length, the highest point being 1,890 feet. The ridge tapers towards the south, finally disappearing altogether so that the land at the south end on Tobago is absolutely flat, the formation at this end being coral. Thus there are two distinct types of scenery in Tobago, the mountains and the flats, both rich in flora and fauna

opposite / Gilpin Waterfall

overleaf / tropical variety

Tobago: Home to one of the World's First Protected Rainforests

TROPISCHE REGENWALD, or "tropical rainforest," is a term attributed to the German plant geographer Alfred Schimper in the late 19th century. But the first legally protected tropical rainforest in the western hemisphere, had already been established in 1776, some hundred years earlier, in Tobago's Main Ridge or Central Forest Reserve.

Tobagonians are justifiably proud of this fact, which many consider the world's first environmental act. However, it did not come easy. Colonial plantation owners saw the forest as lumber. At about that same time, English scientist Stephen Hales had deduced the intimate link between forests and rainfall - if you cut forests down, rainfall stops. Soame Jenyns, an English MP and friend of Hales, realised how important this discovery was and lobbied for a law to protect what is now known as the Main Ridge Forest Reserve. It took him 11 years to convince the powers that be, that cutting down the forest would turn Tobago into a veritable desert and doom its crops. On 13 April 1776 a law was passed to protect the forest forever.

Two hundred years later, despite this knowledge and much more, rainforests the world over are still under siege. We now know the myriad benefit of rainforests to humanity in real and irreplaceable ways. Apart from "creating" rain through evapotranspiration, rainforests act as carbon sinks, absorbing large volumes of carbon dioxide which reduce global warming; they act as water catchments collecting rainwater throughout the year, feeding streams and rivers and providing clean water for millions of people in the tropics; rainforests control soil erosion, breaking up rain with their leaves and binding soil with their roots; the thick green blankets of rainforests create the albedo effect, which decreases global

Clement Williams

Clement Williams

Tobago Tourism Authority

variety of life / a red squirrel and a
tropical caterpillar

warming by reducing the "shininess" of the land and limiting the amount of heat reflected into the atmosphere; and, most well-known, rainforests are the most biologically-diverse ecosystems on earth. They contain over half the estimated 5-10 million plants and animals yet occupy only 6% of the world's surface.

The range of South American rainforest biodiversity is phenomenal. Tobago shares in this natural boon having been attached to the mainland in ancient times, and even shares some species with northern Venezuela that do not exist in Trinidad. It is this diversity, and its ease of accessibility, that sets Tobago's rainforest apart from all others in the Caribbean save Trinidad.

Over 220 species of birds have been recorded in Tobago of which 100 may be spotted in the Reserve. Sadly, several types of animals have become extinct in Tobago, but there still exists mammalian wildlife such as armadillos, agoutis, wild pigs, red squirrels, raccoons and opossums. One can also find several species of non-venomous snakes, and many types of lizards, frogs and bats, including a fish-eating bat. Generally, insect life has been poorly recorded. But as in all rainforests they abound, with many species, no doubt, waiting to be discovered. Plant records are also rare, with the last major tree survey taking place in 1943.

Another factor has recently affected the types of growth associated with the island's rainforest that can't be easily observed elsewhere. Hurricane Flora devastated Tobago's rainforest in 1963. Pockets of old-growth trees survived, but for the most part Flora's terrible winds and destructive rainfall ravaged 75% of the forest. As a result Tobago's rainforest provides a living example of new growth rainforest regenerating in a natural way. Forty-one years on, the lush

ground vegetation and slender trees show a rainforest renewing itself. And in a century or so, unless there is another destructive intervention, there will be huge trees, a dense canopy and minimal ground vegetation. In these times of intense human pressure, and in such a small accessible island, this kind of conservation is very rare indeed.

The Main Ridge Forest Reserve runs along a mountainous ridge along the upper or eastern half of the cigar-shaped island. Here the land rises steeply into the hills and on the other side drops sharply to sandy beaches below. Damp, misty rainforests provide a beacon for enthusiastic naturalists and bird lovers.

There are impressive tracts of rainforest that can be reached by hiking tours that follow some of the old Amerindian trails. One way to get there by car is to take the Rainforest Reserve Road that runs through a mature virgin rainforest reserve from just south of Roxborough through to Bloody Bay. Eventually you'll reach Gilpin Trace, one of the main trails in the Reserve.

Here you'll see Tobago's stratified tropical rainforest, characterised by evergreen woody vegetation with a high, closed canopy 30-50 metres (100-165 feet) up. The emergent layer has the biggest trees that sometimes protrude above the upper canopy. Large lianas, or climbers, are common and can be spotted easily on hilly roads around Castara. Ferns, palms and slow-growing trees that don't need much light dominate the understory layer. On the ground layer there is a profusion of seedlings and herbaceous plants, with many epiphytes (orchids and bromeliads) growing on trunks and branches. There are also numerous refreshing streams and cascading waterfalls to be found throughout the forest and around the island.

top / mangrove swamps behind palm-fringed beaches

middle & above / exploring the variety of Tobago's tropical landscape

Tobago Tourism Authority

Some estimates of world tropical deforestation put loss or degradation of rainforests at around 100,000 sq km (39,000 sq miles) a year. It is difficult to estimate exactly, but suffice it to say the earth's rainforests are under huge and increasing pressure to survive. Many unique rainforest systems have been completely wiped out. The loss of these resources is incalculable. Thankfully, Tobago's little slice of rainforest heaven has been protected for over two centuries and will continue to be protected indefinitely.

Tobago Tourism Authority

opposite / a silk cotton tree

top / a rainforest fern

above / colourful tropical flora

previous pages / the Highlands
Waterfall and some rainforest flora

these and the following pages /
A selection of the flora that can be
found in Tobago's rainforest

top | an old canoe, possibly Amerindian

middle | Arnos Vale nature park

above | the ancient tropical forest on Little Tobago

A History of the 'Tranquil Isle'

I T'S EASY TO GET a sense of history in Tobago, where old sugar mills, forts and plantation great houses dot the landscape. But if you're looking for the facts behind what some still refer to as Robinson Crusoe's island, there are three excellent places to start: the Tobago Museum, housed in the old Barrack Guard House in Fort King George, Scarborough; the delightful First Historical Café, just outside Studley Park on the Windward coast and the vibrant Tobago Heritage Festival, which every July celebrates and helps preserve the island's largely Afro-Creole heritage of story telling and folklore, reel and jig dances and tambrin music at events like the Moriah Wedding, held in authentic village settings.

Nowadays Tobago redefines the concept of laid back, and even Caribbean time seems to move a little slower here, yet there was a period when the comings and goings of European invaders made the "tranquil isle" one of the busiest in the eastern Caribbean and when the phrase "rich as a Tobago planter" gained currency.

The island that Columbus sighted in 1498 and named Assumpcion had first been settled by Arawak speaking Amerindians from South America around 300BC. By the time the first Europeans arrived in the late 16th century, these Tainos had been replaced by the more warlike Kalina or Island Caribs who knew the island as "Tavaco" (the Amerindian for tobacco according to some sources, although others think it refers to a pipe). If you fancy an afternoon's archaeology, there are Amerindian sites at King Peter's, Rockly, Halifax, King's, Queen's, Canoe, Great Courlan and Man O'War bays as well as on Little Tobago and even in the grounds of the Arnos Vale nature park, where

Clement Williams

you can also visit an old slave village and take in a cultural show while indulging in some of the restaurant's highly acclaimed cuisine.

Like their tribesmen throughout the Lesser Antilles, the Tobago Caribs had no intention of handing over their paradise without a fight. They wiped out the first English settlers (1625) and a party of Dutch fared no better in 1628, when a combined Spanish and Carib force from Trinidad arrived in dugout canoes. Although nominally Spanish, the English claimed ownership by virtue of a flag nailed to a tree by some sailors en route to Brazil in 1580, and in one of the most incongruous historical twists Charles I gave Tobago as a christening gift to his godson James Duke of Courlan (modern Latvia) in 1641. The Courlaners who arrived next year found a hot Carib reception, followed by the Dutch who after landing at the site of Scarborough in 1654 and establishing Lampsinburg, captured the Courlaner's Plymouth settlement in 1658 and renamed it Nieuw Vlissingen. Lampsinburg had the distinction of being blown up twice: first by the English in 1666 and then by the French in 1677, when a cannon ball hit the fort's ammunition dump.

Maybe sensing the onset of a feeding frenzy, the Caribs retired north as the full European onslaught began. By the time Tobago was finally ceded to Britain in 1814, it had changed hands an incredible 31 times. The many forts (Milford, Bennett, James, Granby, French, King George) cannon, tombstones and the recently discovered shipwrecks in Scarborough and Roxborough harbours are testimonies to these turbulent times, when if the English, Dutch or French weren't in charge, pirates were.

Following the Dutch seizure of Plymouth in 1658, France's Louis XIV,

Clement Williams

Clement Williams

top / history and culture on display at the Tobago Museum

middle / a guest makes his way to an 'Old Time' or 'Moriah' wedding

above / Old Black Rock Moravian Church, built in 1912

Clement Williams

opposite top / overlooking James Park is the Old Courthouse. His Excellency Governor Sir F P Robinson laid the foundation stone on 23rd April 1821. The building once housed the island's legislative and judiciary and is now the home of the Tobago House of Assembly, the local government of the island

opposite bottom / a cannon at Fort Cambleton, overlooking Pirates Bay

oblivious to the English claim, granted the Dutch control, who were then driven out by the English who in turn were expelled by the French, who promptly burnt the settlement.

Unhappy with French dominance, Britain sent a powerful fleet in 1672, reclaiming the island and establishing a plantation culture driven by African slave labour, producing sugar, cotton and indigo. The Dutch returned a couple of years later, largely dismantling the pioneering British efforts in an attempt to appease other competing colonies. Declared a no-man's land by the 1684 Treaty of Aix La Chapelle, Dutch, French and English settlers co-existed peacefully until once again the island became British in 1762 when the House of Assembly was established and work begun on Fort King George. The first capital was founded in 1762 at Mount St George but was abandoned in 1769 for Scarborough. From hereon the colony began a period of rapid development.

By 1777 some 80 estates were exporting 160,000 gallons of rum, 24,000 cwt of sugar, 1.5m lbs of cotton and 5,000 lbs of indigo. Out of the 1791 population of 15,020, some 14,170 were slaves. Vastly outnumbering the whites, slave revolts were an almost annual affair.

The repercussions of both the French Revolution and the American War of Independence were felt in tiny far-flung Tobago. In 1778 the Americans briefly joined the list of predators and the French returned in 1781. Scarborough was renamed Port Louis and Fort King George became Fort Castries, but as royalism gave way to the republicanism of the French Revolution, in 1790 the French soldiers mutinied, imprisoned their officers and razed Scarborough to the ground.

Clement Williams

Clement Williams

Clement Williams

Clement Williams

top / A disused waterwheel at Speyside - evidence of Tobago's sugar plantation history

above / Fort James Plymouth - named after Jacobus (James) Duke of Courlan.
The present fort was built in the early 1800s and is Tobago's oldest fort

Clement Williams

By 1803 Tobago was finally back in British hands. Initially it prospered but after Emancipation removed its tractable labour force in 1838, it began an economic decline it has never really recovered from. The removal of protective tariffs on sugar dealt a body blow to Tobago's unmechanised industry, compounded by the devastating 1847 hurricane and the collapse of the West India Bank which underwrote the plantations. Sharecropping was introduced with reasonable success until the 1870s when planters began reneging on agreements and labour unrest ignited the 1876 Belmanna Riots which began on the Roxborough Estate.

The planters now thoroughly intimidated, surrendered self-government for Crown Colony status in 1879 and in 1899 Tobago was made a ward of Trinidad, although in 1927 it was granted a single seat on the legislative council. After Independence in 1962 (as part of the twin island state of Trinidad and Tobago) a degree of self sovereignty was restored when the Tobago House of Assembly was reconvened in 1980 and Tobago-born ANR Robinson who served as T&T's prime minister from 1986-91, ensured his island enjoyed a higher profile in the republic.

/ *Simon Lee*

Clement Williams

top / The Tobago House of Assembly

above / A N R Robinson, the first chairman of the Tobago House of Assembly from its inauguration on 4 December 1980 to Dec 1986. He then became Prime Minister and later President of Trinidad and Tobago in 1986. He was succeeded as chairman of the Tobago House of Assembly by Dr Jeff Davidson (Dec 86 to Oct 1989); Lennox Denoon (Nov 1989 to Dec 1996); Hochoy Charles (Dec 1996 to Jan 2001) and Orville London (Feb 2001 to present)

Some Interesting Facts and Amazing Fiction

top / goat racing at Buccoo

above / a silk cotton tree, as fabled in the Gang Gang Sara tale

opposite / tropical water lilies in the Central Forest Reserve

overleaf / Richmond Great House - an elegantly restored plantation house dating from 1766

/ The 14,000 acre **Central Forest Reserve**, established by British colonial authorities on April 13, 1776 "for the preservation of the rains" is the oldest protected rainforest in the western hemisphere

/ **Bloody Bay** on the Leeward coast is named after a battle between English soldiers and slaves in 1771 that turned the blue waters red with the carnage (although some claim the water was stained by red earth deposits)

/ **Man O'War Bay** is the site of buried pirate treasure

/ The Easter Tuesday Buccoo **Goat Races** - a unique sport - were originally introduced by the Barbadian Samuel Callender in 1925

/ The mystery of African slave **Betty Stiven's tomb** in Plymouth lies in the inscription: "What was remarkable about her; she was a mother without knowing it and a wife without letting her husband know it, except by her kind indulgences to him." Possible solutions are that 23 year old Betty was the lover of wealthy Dutch planter Alex Stiven, who raised their child without recognising Betty as the mother; or that the relationship between Betty and Alex was kept secret and when she died in childbirth, Alex commemorated their passion with this cryptic message.

/ **Richmond Great House**, near Glamorgan on the Windward coast, was built in the 18th century and restored by Professor Hollis Lynch who now runs it as a guest house and restaurant and home to his extensive collection of African art and textiles.

/ **Bacolet Bay Beach** was the location for the movie *Swiss Family Robinson* and a favourite frolicking spot for the Beatles in the late 1960s and early 70s.

/ **Gang Gang Sara** the obeah woman of folklore is believed to be buried in Golden Lane. She flew from Africa to Les Coteaux searching for her family and found them in Golden Lane, where she also found and married her sweetheart Tom. When he died she climbed a silk cotton tree ready for the return flight to Africa but found she'd lost the art of flight through eating salt.

Simon Lee

old time transport

African-Creole Roots Culture

"Jackass say world nuh level"

THIS TOBAGONIAN proverb which roughly translates as 'life just ain't fair', transforms a tired truism into a memorable soundbyte. There are many more such proverbs, or parables as the old folk call them: 'Cockroach doh sleep wit fowl'; 'Every barn hog get it Saturday' and the unforgettable 'If sugar was shit I woulda stand up' which of course means - some things are virtually impossible.

These are all reminders of Tobago's traditional folk wisdom soaked in earthy humour and an oral culture as old as its chequered history. Parables are part of everyday life, as much a relic of old world style as the formal greetings you'll encounter on any country road, or hillside village.

Tobago traditions reflect the island's sometimes baffling position, poised between its past of subsistence farmers and small fishing communities largely descended from African slaves, and a future of upscale tourist development. On this tiny island the eighteenth century collides with the 21st: internet resort bookings and helicopter tours versus African ancestor worship and folktales.

There are entirely modern traditions like Sunday School in Buccoo, a street party with steelband and DJs, unashamed fun tourist entertainment and then revived customs like the Old Time Wedding, a prominent feature of July's Heritage Festival.

One custom which you're likely to come across on a daily basis from Store Bay in the west to Charlotteville in the east is 'pulling seine', the communal retrieving of fishing nets cast close to shore. While there are fish in the sea, Tobagonians will pull their seines and this is one custom you'll be more than

Charles Scott

welcome to join in, as every pair of hands is needed to pull in the hoop of fish-heavy, lead-weighted net.

Once they've spotted shoals of small fish like sprats, jacks or even larger bonito, fishermen in boats drop the net in a circle from the shore. Any and everybody can help to pull in the catch, part of which they can claim as payment for their effort. This is not only practical in terms of labour but part of the old tradition of 'Len han' common throughout the Caribbean, a direct descendant of the co-operative work ethic of African villages, which the slaves brought with them and put to good use after Emancipation: building houses or boats, clearing land for cultivation, planting and harvesting.

The First Historical Café and Bar on the Windward Road outside Studley Park provides an ideal quick fix of Tobago history and traditions. While the Atlantic with all its historical associations washes the shore you can scan the wall displays which cover everything from traditional food and drink ("chocolate tea - made from freshly ground cocoa, flavoured with cinnamon, cow's milk and bay leaf"; bake with all the ingredients for bread minus the "raising agent") to folk dances ("The Reel or Jumbie, a purely African ritual dance which led to possession by an ancestor who brought messages"; "The Bongo - danced at 9 night wakes as grief therapy").

Many of Tobago's older traditions were saved for posterity thanks to the late JD Elder, a noted anthropologist/ethnomusicologist, who insisted they were incorporated in the Heritage Festival, when it was established in the 1980s. The festival has since acted as a focus for unearthing and reviving dormant folk culture. The common feature of these older traditions is the mixing of African

Clement Williams

top / the tradition of 'pulling seine'

above / a young girl dressed for the heritage festival

dressed to impress / a guest at a
Moriah Wedding

and European styles and customs. Among the core events which are staged in authentic village settings are the Moriah Wedding with its groom in stove pipe and tail coat, bride with trousseau on head, the procession accompanied by fiddler and tambrin drummers. Here the costuming may be European but the music moves to distinctly African rhythms. Plymouth stages an old time carnival with African stickfighting and masquerade characters with English titles like Duke, Valentine, Show Boy and Commander who parade and dance in decorated European top hats but whose origins are thought to lie in the street festivals of Nigeria. They are joined by Ju Ju warriors, Jab Jabs and devils dressed in satin, reminiscent of old English clowns.

Bethel and Plymouth are also home to famous Speech bands, an entirely unique Tobago tradition linked to carnival. A cast of costumed characters including Creator, Sealey, The King, Hero Conqueror, The Duke of Wellington, The Doctor, My Boy Pompey speechify in rhyme, a form resembling old English Mummers plays but which obviously owes much to the vibrant African oral tradition.

The Heritage Festival's Folk Fiesta staged at Signal Hill showcases dancing, singing and drumming and a tambrin band competition. Tobagonian music and dance is quite distinct from that of its larger sister island with its more cosmopolitan influences. While some Creole dances like the Belé and Piqué are found in both islands, the Reel and Jig and the accompanying tambrin music are uniquely Tobagonian. Tambrin (from tambourine) is quintessential Tobago music. It is driven by three shallow goatskin 'tambrin' drums: the cutter (high pitch), roller (rhythm) and boom (bass). The drums provide an African basis for the lead instrument the fiddle and the added percussion of a steel triangle.

Tambrin bands dominated village social events (processions, weddings, boat christenings, harvest festivals) and islandwide festivals right up to the 1960s and the advent of the DJ. Contemporary bands include The Professionals and Unity from Mt Thomas, Cateson from Mt St George and Plymouth's Royal Sweet Fingers.

Tambrin was traditionally used for both adapted European dances like the quadrille, polka, waltz, Lancers and the South American pasea and for the African derived ritual dances-the Reel and Jig. These last two dances are evidence of Tobago's African roots, traditions which survived colonial oppression by camouflaging themselves in the European form of British sailors' dances.

The Reel, Jig, Saraka from Pembroke and even the Belé are dances invoking the spirits of the ancestors and dead, a tactic for survival, inspiration and resistance since slavery days. The ceremony of pouring libation of white rum and water in the road at the beginning of a Reel, inviting the ancestors into the yard parallels the ceremony for Papa Legba, guardian of the gate, a prerequisite for any Vodou ceremony in Haiti.

As the dance progressed spirits would manifest themselves 'riding' or possessing dancers through whom they revealed messages, suppressed information or the

Clement Williams

cause of sickness, entrapment or other problems. The Reel was danced on many occasions-at the annual wake for the dead, a boat launching or seine hanging, during times of sickness or recovery, evil or hardship and on bachelor's night before a wedding.

African influences survive in other traditions: folklore, agricultural superstitions and bush medicine. There are the tales of Wawa Douglas and Conga Brown who when beaten by the slavemaster, magically transferred the lashes to the planter's wife and Congo Ellis who because he didn't eat salt was able to fly back to Africa.

While gardeners wouldn't dream of planting if a funeral was taking place in the village, they would make sure to bathe before entering a yam plot as these tubers are regarded as particularly sensitive. Folk cures include mat root for diabetes and snake bites; bamboo leaf for fevers, pneumonia or strokes and lizard grass for gastroenteritis.

/ *Simon Lee*

traditional beat / tambrin
drummers at a Moriah Wedding

The 'Moriah' or 'Old Time' Tobago Wedding

opposite / Old Time bride and groom

above / guests at the Moriah Wedding

"THERE IS NOTHING like the 'Old Time' Tobago wedding!" Miss Ruth, an 89-year old Moriah Villager, stoutly asserted. She had just received an invitation to attend a wedding. Wedding invitations annoyed her. "I feel insulted!" she said.

"Tobagonians were not accustomed to wedding invitations, but things have changed now," Miss Ruth lamented. "In my day, if you wanted, you just attended any wedding on the island. Let me tell you about the first wedding that I 'walked'."

I was 17 years old when Miss Vida's second daughter got married. I wanted to 'walk' the wedding but I did not know whether Tan-Tan would allow me. Since I was a little child I stood at the side of the road and watched many wedding processions up and down the village. This time I wanted to be a part of the celebrations.

I decided to make it difficult for Tan-Tan to refuse to send me. So, a week before the wedding I got out of bed one hour earlier than usual and began my chores. I even did some of Pappy's chores. I knew that Pappy would not object to me going to the wedding, but - oh...Tan-Tan!

Three days before the wedding, the haunting strains of the tambrin and fiddle began to invade my mind. I would sit and daydream of the procession wending its way through Kitty Bamboo Gully all the way up to Lincoln Gap. I could even hear the tramp, tramp, tramp of the ladies' stone-crushers along the gravel path as they danced the brush-back. I visualized the men decked in black top hats, scissors tail coats flying in the breeze; their black umbrellas held upright, as they matched paces with the women. I yearned to be a part of this procession.

With determination I got up from the old tree stump and rushed inside the shed. I gathered all Tan-Tan and Pappy's dirty garden clothes, packed them in a big basin, grabbed the scrubbing board, a corn stick and a bar of blue soap and headed for the river. Three hours later I returned to the house with my laundry perched on top of my head. Tan-Tan actually came out to meet me. 'Child, you working so hard; come inside for a cup of rainwater and a bowl of susumba soup before you hang out the clothes,' she invited me.

opposite / dancing the brush-back
on the road

above / bride and groom lead
wedding guests

'Yes Tan-Tan,' I replied.'Tan-Tan I want to go to the wedding on
Saturday?' 'Yes Doris, let the child go to the wedding,' Pappy answered
from the side of the shed. At last, it was settled; I would be 'WALKING'
the wedding.

The day before the wedding I washed and cork-screwed my hair,
sunned out my yellow taffeta dress, polished my white sling-back stone-
crusher and borrowed a hat from Netty.

There was no comparison between that wedding and what they are
calling wedding these days. No, I will not go to another wedding if they
are driving in cars! Tell me what kind of marriage will the bride have -
with no one carrying her trunk, the breadfruit or the coalpot?

Imagine, now you have to carry your invitation to get into the reception
and after waiting hours you are given a little bit of food - and nothing
to carry home! The real Tobago wedding was a free-for-all. The 'marish
and the parish' was always welcomed. Everyone got enough food to eat
and to carry home. In those days the men killed and cooked the pigs,
the goats and the yard fowls and made the dumplings. The women
turned the coo-coo and cooked the callaloo, the rice and the ground
provisions.

We did not have caterers then. Who would pay strangers to cook for
their wedding! And what do they serve? A spoon of Spanish rice, a
sliver of macaroni pie, one piece of baked chicken and a leaf of lettuce
with a slice of tomato; no ginger-beer, no sorrel, no mauby! You ever
hear more? A wedding is supposed to be an occasion for everyone to
eat, drink and be merry. Tobago has really changed!"

Indeed, Tobago has changed. Though the Ole' Time Wedding is not as
popular as it once was, it still enjoys a place of prominence in Tobago's
annual Heritage Festival. The Ole' Time Wedding has given way to
conventional weddings and even some unorthodox ceremonies have
taken place on the island from time to time. The mandatory three-day
residency status on Tobago before being married has attracted many
visitors to the island for their wedding/honeymoon vacation. Imagine
strolling around the picturesque Fort King George and being politely
approached to be a witness to a Swedish couple's marriage ceremony.
A few steps away, the blushing bride with fresh flower bouquet, in
white skirt and shirt and a smiling groom, decked in short-sleeved shirt,
neck tie, short trousers and a pair of slippers, wait expectantly with the
Preacher, while the other witness walks you back to the scene.

On the other hand, some of Tobago's visitors indulge in rather lavish
wedding functions. An Italian/English couple recently tied the knot on
Pigeon Point, the island's most popular beach resort. The groom and
guests waited excitely while the bride arrived side-saddled atop a

garlanded mare through coconut palms beside the tranquil turquoise sea.

An American/Puerto Rican couple chose one of the island's popular resorts close to Plymouth for their celebration. They wanted all their wedding functions to be held on the beach.

On the wedding eve they requested a beach-side flambeau-lit dinner party. As the evening sun sank into the horizon the beach was transformed into a breath-taking nocturnal scenery. Shaded candles formed a twinkling mosaic along the beachfront and about fifty lighted flambeaus encircled the large dinner table. Soon, champagne and the infectious music of the local folk performers drew everyone to their feet. Shoes were kicked into the sand as the party moved to rhythm of the Tobago beat. That night was long with the wedding day being even longer.

"I heard all about that one," Miss Ruth quipped. "It was a good function. That is what we called the Bachelor's Night Party. One element was missing though the whole of Plymouth should have been allowed to attend."

| Sandie Hendrix

opposite top / happy couple at Moriah Wedding

opposite bottom / wedding guests getting down old time style

top / wedding procession arrives for the feast at Moriah

above / Moriah maid of honour carries wedding cake aloft

top / heating a tambrin
goatskin drum

middle / tambrin drummer
on the road

above / Tan Tan keeping time

opposite / thirsty work - a carnival
dancer stops for refreshment

Tobago Fest

THIS RECENT ADDITION to Tobago's cultural calendar (end of September) gives carnival lovers a second chance to jump up in a Trini style carnival with strong Tobagonian flavours. Of course there's the added bonus that once the festivities are over, there are a range of beaches close at hand for rest and recuperation.

Most of the main features of Trini carnival have been incorporated into Tobago Fest: Jouvert (the raucous dawnbreak street jump up which heralds the beginning of the fete); the Parade of the Bands featuring popular masquerade bands from Trinidad; soca and calypso shows and steelband competition; Fest Queen and talent contest; night mas (which allows the party to continue under the stars in cooler temperatures) and unlimited street parties.

Along with these imports from the sister isle Tobago contributes some traditional elements from its own carnival including the Speech bands of Bethel and Plymouth and mas bands extravagantly costumed as royalty or in old fashioned European formal dress.

For visitors unable to make the mother of all carnivals earlier in the year Tobago Fest is both a mini introduction and a chance to see Tobagonians at their festive best.

Charles Scott

Clement Williams

Simon Lee

top and opposite / heritage festival dancers

above / bongo dance at Whim wake

right / dancers of Rhythmic Vibration

overleaf / old time carnival with red and blue devils

Clement Williams

Clement Williams

playing with fire / carnival devils

Stephen Broadbridge

Stephen Broadbridge

top / limbo dancing

left / internationally-renowned singer and songwriter Stevie Wonder, performing at Tobago's Jazz Festival

above / a heritage festival dancer

A Day at the Races

Crab Racing / among Tobago's unique customs are the goat and crab races (above), traditionally held at Buccoo on Easter Tuesday, which has become a Tobago public holiday. If the goat races are sometimes amusing, the crab race which follows is usually hysterical both for spectators and frustrated crab handlers. Attached to a string and guided by small sticks, the crustaceans are usually unmoved by the desperate yells of the humans or the incentive of choice morsels supposed to keep them on course for the black and white chequered flag. Most either back off the few yards of track, or scuttle sideways for the nearby sea.

T IS POPULAR and fun and for nearly 80 years, Buccoo, a small village on Tobago's southwestern side, has been conducting goat racing. Started in 1925 by the late Samuel Callender, a Barbadian native, this was in fact the poor man's equivalent to the horse races, which was reserved for the local gentry at the time. Horse racing occupied Easter Monday on the calendar and the following Tuesday was declared 'Easter Tuesday' in Tobago and dedicated to the racing of goats for the entertainment of the 'lower classes'.

The races were held on one of the village streets, now called Chance Street, but were relocated when the road was paved and the area developed. The next venue known as the 'Battery' proved to be an unpopular location due to the proximity of overhanging cliffs at the finish line. The event then changed locations for the final time 21 years ago to its current venue neighbouring the Buccoo Beach facility. Since its inception, the event has been planned and organised by a sub-committee of the Buccoo Village Council now referred to as the Buccoo Goat Race Festival Committee. Although Easter Tuesday is 'officially' Goat Races Day in Tobago, the activity now occurs more regularly on the entertainment calendar at events such as the Tobago Heritage Festival. The sport has been adopted by the nearby village of Mt Pleasant for the past few years.

Strength and speed are required of a good racing goat and this is achieved by the hard work and dedication of the owners, trainers and jockeys. The animals are trained for at least two months prior to racing and during this period they learn to walk at increasing speeds until they're running in front of the trainer with a rope round their neck as on race day. A swimming routine to build muscles is also a critical part of the training as is diet. It is thought that nanny

Clement Williams

goats are better runners. However, billy goats are the preferred choice since they live longer. A racing goat can live as long as 13 years given the correct care and attention.

The jockeys are a critical link between winners and losers as their speed must be akin to that of their charges. Often a goat will outrun the jockey and become disqualified. Therefore the training, diet and other physical activities are also regulated during the time leading up to the races for this test of speed and endurance.

Like horse racing, classification is important to the stakeholders. The Buccoo Goat Race Festival Committee uses these classifications: *C2 - First time runners, C1 - Runners from the previous year, B - Running for the past two years, A - Most experienced runners.*

The event starts with a somewhat noisy street parade where booths offering crafts, T-shirts, food and drink line the route. Many residents also open their homes to the visitors and provide delicious local cuisine for the occasion.

The Goat Race Festival has now become a major event in Tobago's tourism calendar. The Tobago House of Assembly's Department of Tourism as well as the Tourism and Industrial Development Company of Trinidad and Tobago (TIDCO) have sponsored the races over the years. The Goat Race Festival has evolved into a truly family affair where generations meet through tradition and visitors caught up in the festive atmosphere become honorary Tobagonians for a day.

| *Dextor Trim & Lois Solomon*

top | Goat Racing at Buccoo, traditionally held on Easter Tuesday

above | a potential champion

top and above / fishing boats and nets at Charlotteville

opposite / dividing up the catch

Agriculture and Fishing

C ULTIVATING the land and fishing the sea have a history, stretching back over 300 years in Tobago. Sugarcane was the main product of the slavery era, when the tradition of small-scale gardening was also established-slaves were given small plots of land on which to grow their own provisions as supplements to the meagre diets supplied by the masters. Following the decline of the sugar industry in the late nineteenth century, cocoa became the main crop until the 1980s, closely followed by coconut and its derivative, copra.

Since the 1980s domestic agriculture has dominated, continuing the Afro-Creole tradition of self-sufficiency. The main products are fruit, vegetables, roots and tubers (including yam, sweet potato, dasheen and eddoe) and livestock (goats, pigs, cattle, poultry) most of which goes to local markets or to the tourist industry. The Blenheim Sheep Multiplication and Research Project is recognised internationally as a centre for hair sheep development.

A recent innovation has been cut flower production (anthuriums, ginger lilies, heliconias, orchids and tropical foliage) for export to America and Europe, a market which now nets more than TT$10 million annually. Bee keeping is another developing sector, especially as Tobago is free of the pests, diseases and the Africanised bee which limit honey production elsewhere.

Fishing has always played a major role in Tobago life and economy due to the wide variety and abundance of marine life. Besides supporting coastal villages, fishing now supplies a number of processing plants which export to local, regional and international markets.

As tourism becomes an increasingly important sector of the economy, agricultural initiatives are being planned to service the new industry.

above / a happy sport fisherman displays his catch

left / fishing pirogues ready for the next trip

opposite / a fisherman cleans his catch

Tobago Tourism Authority

opposite top / pulling in the seine

opposite bottom / young fisherman casts his net

tropical produce / breadfruit (above) and one of Tobago's major crops, cocoa (right)

overleaf / sorting and drying cocoa and the traditional cocoa dance

Tobago Tourism Authority

Clement Williams

Clement Williams

Health and Education

H EALTH CARE throughout Tobago has benefited from recent initiatives to decentralise health services and improve primary health care to all communities, with particular emphasis on maternal and child health.

In addition to the Tobago regional hospital in Scarborough, the Seventh Day Adventist hospital on Milford Road and the Scarborough Medical Associates private clinic, there are now a number of health centres in towns like Plymouth and Roxborough and rural villages like Moriah and Les Coteaux.

Tobagonians have a healthy respect for education and the island has produced some internationally acclaimed scholars including anthropologist and ethnomusicologist, the late JD Elder.

There are a large number of primary schools (Government, Anglican, Methodist, Roman Catholic, Seventh Day Adventist and private) as well as eight secondary schools. The T&T Hospitality and Tourism Institute has a campus in Scarborough. For tertiary level education Tobagonians either travel to the sister island's UWI campus at St Augustine or go abroad.

opposite / a healthy bunch of bananas, also called green figs

teaching and healing / children graduating from Kindergarden (top), the new Canaan Health Centre (middle) and the Medical Transcriptionist Building (above)

Tobago : propre,
verte et paisible

L'ÎLE en forme de cigare que les Amérindiens baptisèrent d'après la feuille
qu'ils aimaient fumer se trouve à 34 km au nord-est de son île súur, la
Trinité. Elle fit tant l'admiration de Christophe Colomb qu'il l'appela
« Bellaforma ».

L'île tranquille de Tobago, entourée de récifs coralliens, mesure 34 km de long
sur 11 km de large. Au sud-ouest, un plateau corallien s'élève en pente douce
jusqu'à une crête de collines volcaniques atteignant 576 m d'altitude. Dans la
moitié est, les plages de sable blanc et les baies et petites anses isolées de la
côte sous le vent ou côte des Caraïbes, ainsi que le littoral rocheux de la côte
Atlantique, du côté du vent, cèdent la place à une forêt tropicale humide dense
(la plus ancienne forêt protégée de l'hémisphère occidental) qui recouvre les
montagnes que traversent des vallées baignées de rivières et des cascades en
direction du sud.

Jusqu'à une époque géologique récente, l'île de Tobago était rattachée au
continent sud-américain. C'est pourquoi elle regorge d'espèces végétales et
animales uniques à l'île mais aussi provenant du continent, et dont le nombre
est disproportionné par rapport à sa superficie : 210 espèces d'oiseaux, 123
espèces de papillons, 24 espèces de serpents (tous inoffensifs), 17 espèces de
chauves-souris, 16 espèces de lézards, 14 espèces de grenouilles et 12 espèces
de mammifères (dont le tatou, l'agouti, l'opossum et le pécari).

Habitée à l'origine par les Amérindiens, Tobago fut plus tard un pion qui
changea souvent de camp sur l'échiquier colonial européen. C'est de l'actuelle
Lettonie qu'arrivèrent les premiers colons pour s'établir sur l'île en 1642. Ils
furent chassés en 1658 par les Hollandais, qui furent suivis par des vagues
successives d'invasions françaises et anglaises jusqu'à ce que l'île soit cédée à la

Grande-Bretagne en 1802 par le Traité de Paris. Tobago devint colonie de la Couronne britannique en 1877 avant d'être réunie en 1888 à la Trinité, à la suite de l'effondrement de l'industrie sucrière, pour former une unité politique.

La majorité des 55 000 habitants de l'île sont des descendants d'esclaves africains qui furent transportés jusqu'ici, à partir de la fin du XVIIe siècle, pour qu'ils travaillent dans des plantations de canne à sucre, de coton et d'indigo. Depuis plus récemment, des habitants de la Trinité (pour la plupart des marchands, des commerçants, des personnes travaillant dans l'industrie de l'accueil et des hommes d'affaires d'origine indienne) ainsi que des expatriés, attirés par un style de vie décontracté, ont donné à la population une nouvelle dimension.

Pour ce qui est de la culture, les racines de la population de Tobago sont strictement antillaises d'origine africaine, contrairement au caractère cosmopolite de la Trinité. Les croyances et le folklore africains continuent de prospérer à l'ombre des fromagers, dans les communautés à flanc de coteau et, dans la musique folklorique, le tambourin vibre sur un rythme africain. On peut admirer certaines des plus belles traditions africaines dans leur cadre villageois authentique durant la Fête du patrimoine, qui a lieu chaque année en juillet ; mais à tout moment de l'année, on peut tomber sur une fête de la moisson, une danse « reel » dédiée aux ancêtres ou un autre type de fête.

L'industrie lourde étant cantonnée à la Trinité, la nature, à Tobago, est restée en grande partie intacte. De nombreux habitants de l'île vivent de la pêche ou des cultures de leur jardin (agriculture de subsistance), mais ils sont de plus en plus nombreux à travailler dans le tourisme en commercialisant le plus précieux atout de l'île : sa nature splendide.

Tobago est le meilleur site de plongée du sud-est des Caraïbes. Sous la surface

de la mer, de magnifiques récifs coralliens qui s'élèvent en pente douce, des falaises sous-marines vertigineuses et des formations volcaniques offrent de superbes plongées aux novices et aux plongeurs expérimentés. Grâce à sa situation privilégiée - au point de rencontre de l'eau provenant de l'Orénoque avec l'océan Atlantique et la mer des Caraïbes - ses eaux sont riches en nutriments et grouillantes de vie : près de 300 espèces de coraux durs, toutes sortes d'éponges, des myriades de poissons tropicaux et de gros animaux marins tels que baleines, requins, dauphins, les rares raies manta, calmars et tortues.

Même si Scarborough est la capitale nationale de l'île, le petit village de pêcheurs de Speyside est devenu la capitale de la plongée. Sa diversité de sites et les multiples courants de marée qui entourent les îlots côtiers offrent de superbes plongées dérivantes. Bien qu'établie seulement dans les années 1980, l'industrie de la plongée est gérée par des professionnels selon des normes de sécurité internationales, et Scarborough possède une chambre de décompression que l'on peut utiliser gratuitement.

Sur l'eau, tous les sports nautiques imaginables sont proposés - de la voile en Hobie-Cat au kite-surf, en passant par la pêche au gros - et ceux qui préfèrent une approche moins dynamique aimeront observer les récifs assis dans un bateau à fond de verre.

Sur la terre ferme, Tobago attire depuis longtemps les ornithologues, les naturalistes et les écotouristes (dont David Attenborough, mondialement connu, qui a filmé à Tobago une partie de sa série d'émissions pour la télévision «Trials of Life»), qui veulent voir l'emblématique cocrico, faire des randonnées dans la réserve, escalader les cascades ou regarder les tortues

pondre la nuit sur la plage. Au lieu de la voiture, le VTT est une façon très agréable et stimulante de visiter l'île.

Après un magnifique coucher de soleil tropical, les visiteurs seront surpris de voir combien les soirées sur l'île sont animées, avec bien souvent la culture locale en vedette. La fête « Sunday School » qui a lieu sur la plage de Buccoo chaque dimanche est devenue une institution pour les habitants de l'île et les visiteurs, tout comme les courses de chèvres et de crabes uniques en leur genre qui se déroulent à Pâques, ainsi que le carnaval de Tobago (Tobago Fest).

L'économie repose sur le tourisme et l'immobilier, l'énergie étant désormais sérieusement envisagée comme une possibilité de diversification. Le développement immobilier est activement encouragé et les incitations à l'investissement (telles que l'exemption de droits de douane sur les matériaux de construction et l'équipement lié au tourisme importés) ont contribué au lancement de nombreux nouveaux projets sur l'île (grands complexes hôteliers, construction de villas et deux nouvelles galeries marchandes).

Les visiteurs qui ont l'intention d'effectuer des investissements à Tobago bénéficieront non seulement de ces exemptions, mais aussi de la quote-part immobilière, qui leur permet d'être propriétaires de 2 hectares de terrain à des fins commerciales, même sans avoir le statut de résident. Pour ce qui est du développement de la main-d'úuvre, le campus de Tobago de l'Institut de formation aux métiers de l'accueil et du tourisme de Trinité-et-Tobago propose des formations aux métiers manuels, à la cuisine, à l'hôtellerie ainsi qu'à la gestion touristique et l'organisation de voyages.

En séjournant ici, vous découvrirez vite pourquoi les habitants de l'île disent « Tobago sweet » (Tobago la douce).

Tobago: Sauber,
grün und beschaulich

DIE WIE eine Zigarre geformte Insel, die von den Indianern nach dem Blatt der Tabakpflanze benannt wurde, und die Kolumbus so bezauberte, dass er sie „Bellaforma" taufte, liegt 34 km nordöstlich ihrer Schwesterinsel Trinidad.

Von Korallenriffen umgeben, bildet das 34 km lange und 11 km breite Tobago eine Oase der Ruhe. Sein tief liegendes südwestliches Korallenplateau geht allmählich in einen zentralen Kamm vulkanischer Berge über, dessen maximale Höhe ca. 576 Meter beträgt. Auf der östlichen Hälfte der Insel werden die weißen Sandstrände, einsamen Buchten und Meeresarme der leewärtigen bzw. karibischen Küste und die felsige Uferlandschaft der luvwärtigen Atlantikseite von dichtem Regenwald (dem ältesten geschützten Wald in der westlichen Hemisphäre) abgelöst, der das Hochland bedeckt und von Flusstälern und gen Süden strömenden Wasserfällen durchzogen ist.

Bis in relativ jüngster geologischer Zeit war Tobago Teil des südamerikanischen Festlands. Infolgedessen besitzt es eine reiche, sowohl festlands- als auch inseltypische Flora und Fauna, die in keinem Verhältnis zu seiner Größe steht: 210 Vogelarten, 123 Schmetterlingsarten, 24 Schlangenarten (alle harmlos), 17 Fledermausarten, 16 Eidechsenarten, 14 Froscharten und 12 Säugetierarten (u.a. Gürteltier, Agouti-Katze, Opossum und Pekari).

Das ursprünglich von amerikanischen Indianern bewohnte Tobago wurde schon früh zu einem Spielball der europäischen Kolonisationsmächte. Als erste kamen Kolonisten aus dem heutigen Lettland, die sich 1642 auf Tobago niederließen, jedoch 1658 von den Holländern vertrieben wurden. Es schlossen sich mehrere Wellen von französischen und englischen Invasionen an, bis die Insel schließlich

Tobago Tourism Authority

1802, im Vertrag von Paris, Großbritannien zugesprochen wurde. Tobago wurde 1877 eine britische Kronkolonie und, nach dem Zusammenbruch der Zuckerindustrie, 1888 mit Trinidad zu einer politischen Einheit zusammengefasst.

Die Mehrheit der 55.000 Einwohner Tobagos stammt von afrikanischen Sklaven ab, die vom späten 17. Jahrhundert an hierher transportiert wurden, um auf den Zucker, Baumwoll- und Indigoplantagen zu arbeiten. Vom entspannt-lockeren Lebensstil der Insel angezogen, haben sich in den letzten Jahren aber auch zahlreiche Trinidader (hauptsächlich Handels- und Gastronomiebeschäftigte ostindischen Ursprungs) und andere Ausländer auf Tobago niedergelassen, was der Bevölkerung eine weitere Dimension gegeben hat.

Von der Kultur her sind Tobagos Wurzeln jedoch - im Gegensatz zur kosmopolitischen Vielfalt Trinidads - streng afrikanisch-karibisch. Im Schatten der Kapokbäume florieren in den Hügeldörfern weiterhin afrikanische Folklore und Glaubensvorstellungen und trommeln die Tambrins afrikanische Rhythmen. Beim alljährlichen Heritage Festival werden jeden Juli einige der besten afrikanischen Traditionen in ihren authentischen Dorfumgebungen vorgeführt; doch zu jeder Zeit des Jahres kann man unvermutet auf Leichenfeiern, Erntefeste oder Reels (den Ahnen geweihte Tänze) stoßen.

Da die Schwerindustrie ganz auf Trinidad konzentriert ist, konnte Tobago weitgehend unverdorben bleiben. Viele Inselbewohner leben vom Fischfang oder Kleinanbau, doch immer mehr arbeiten auch in der Tourismusbranche, wo sie den wertvollsten Schatz der Insel vermarkten - ihre atemberaubende Natur.

Tobago ist das Top-Tauchrevier der südöstlichen Karibik. Unter der Wasseroberfläche bieten sanft abfallende, unberührte Korallenriffe, steile Unterwasserkliffe und Vulkanformationen faszinierende Taucherlebnisse für Tauchanfänger und Fortgeschrittene. Die glückliche Lage der Insel an genau dem Punkt, wo der Ausfluss aus dem Orinoco-Delta, der Atlantische Ozean und die Karibische See aufeinandertreffen, begünstigt durch nährstoffhaltiges Wasser eine reiche Unterwasserlebewelt: nahezu 300 Arten von Hartkorallen, eine breite Vielfalt von Schwämmen, Myriaden von tropischen Fischen sowie größere Meerestiere wie Wale, Haie, Delphine, seltene Mantarochen, Tintenfische und Schildkröten.

Während Scarborough die Hauptstadt der Insel ist, hat sich das kleine Fischerdorf Speyside zu seiner Tauchhauptstadt entwickelt - mit verschiedenen Tauchrevieren und Gezeitenströmen um die vorgelagerten Inseln, die hervorragendes Drift Diving ermöglichen. Die hiesige Tauchindustrie entstand zwar erst in den 80er Jahren, wird aber professionell nach internationalen Sicherheitstandards gemanagt, und Scarborough verfügt über eine kostenlose Dekompressionskammer.

Auf dem Wasser werden alle nur erdenklichen Sportarten angeboten - von Hobie-Cat Segeln über Drachensurfen bis Game Fishing. Wer er lieber geruhsamer hat, kann die Riffe aber auch von einem Glasbodenboot aus erkunden.

Tobago ist schon lange ein beliebtes Reiseziel für Ornithologen, Naturforscher und Ökotouristen (u.a. den international angesehenen David Attenborough, der hier einen Teil seiner Fernsehserie „Trials of Life" filmte), die den Cocrico, Tobagos Nationalvogel, erspähen, im Forest Reserve durch den Regenwald wandern, Wasserfälle bezwingen oder bei Nacht auf dem Strand nistende

Tobago Tourism Authority

Schildkröten beobachten wollen. Radtouren per Mountainbike sind eine ausgezeichnete, energievolle Alternative zu Autofahrten.

Nach einem wunderbaren tropischen Sonnenuntergang erwartet die Besucher ein überraschend vielseitiges Nachtleben, oft voller Lokalkolorit. Die wöchentliche Sunday School Beach Party in Buccoo ist zur festen Institution für Einheimische und Besucher geworden - ebenso wie die unvergleichlichen Ziegen- und Krabbenrennen zu Ostern und Tobagos eigener Karneval, das „Tobago Fest"

Die Wirtschaft Tobagos wird vom Tourismus und von Grundstücksgeschäften angetrieben, doch Energiegewinnung gilt heute als eine ernsthafte Diversifizierungsmöglichkeit. Grundstückserschließungen werden aktiv unterstützt, und Investitionsanreize wie Zollbefreiung für importierte Baumaterialien und mit der Touristik verbundene Ausrüstungen haben zu vielen neuen Bauprojekten auf der Insel geführt, inkl. große Hotelkomplexe, Villendörfer und zwei neue Einkaufszentren.

Besucher, die auf Tobago investieren wollen, profitieren nicht nur von diesen Steuerbefreiungen sondern auch von einer Liegenschaftenquote, die ihnen, selbst ohne Einwohnerstatus, den Besitz von bis zu 2 Hektar Land für gewerbliche Zwecke gestattet. Für die Ausbildung der Arbeiterschaft bietet der Tobago-Campus des „Trinidad and Tobago Hospitality and Tourism Training Institute" Programme in Handwerk, Kochkunst, Hotel- und Tourbetrieb und Touristikmanagement an.

Verbringen Sie etwas Zeit bei uns und lassen Sie sich zeigen, warum die Inselbewohner vom „süßen Tobago" sprechen!

Tobago: Pulita,
Verde e Tranquilla

L'ISOLA A FORMA di sigaro che gli amerindi battezzarono con il nome della foglia che amavano tanto fumare, e che impressionò tanto Colombo che la chiamò "Bellaforma", giace a 34 km a nord est dell'isola sorella di Trinidad.

Lunga 34 km e larga 11 km, Tobago è un'isola tranquilla e circondata da barriere coralline. La pianura corallina sudoccidentale sale progressivamente fino a una cresta di monti vulcanici che raggiunge 576 metri al centro dell'isola. Dalla parte orientale vi sono le spiagge di sabbia bianca con baie e insenature nascoste della costa di sottovento o dei Caraibi e il litorale roccioso dell'Atlantico di sopravento. Partendo da qui ci si addentra in una foresta tropicale (la più antica foresta protetta dell'emisfero occidentale) che ricopre gli altipiani intersecati dalle valli dei fiumi e dalle cascate di acqua che scorre verso il sud.

In tempi geologici recenti, Tobago faceva parte della terraferma sudamericana. Di conseguenza gode di una grande abbondanza di specie animali e vegetali originarie sia della terraferma che dell'isola stessa e che è del tutto sproporzionata alle dimensioni dell'isola: 210 specie di uccelli, 123 specie di farfalle, 24 tipi di serpenti (tutti innocui), 17 specie di pipistrelli, 16 specie di lucertole, 14 specie di rane e 12 tipi di mammiferi (compresi l'armadillo, l'agouti, l'opossum e il pecari).

Popolata all'origine dagli amerindi, Tobago diventò una pedina ripetutamente scambiata sulla scacchiera coloniale europea. I primi ad arrivare furono coloni provenienti dall'odierna Lettonia, che vi si stabilirono nel 1642. Furono cacciati nel 1658 dagli olandesi, ai quali seguirono successive invasioni di francesi e inglesi, finché l'isola venne ceduta alla Gran Bretagna nel 1802 con il Trattato di

Clement Williams

Parigi. Tobago diventò una colonia della corona britannica nel 1877 e, dopo il
crollo dell'industria dello zucchero, venne unita a Trinidad per formare una
singola unità politica nel 1888.

La maggioranza della popolazione di 55.000 persone è composta da discendenti
degli schiavi africani trasportati per lavorare nelle piantagioni di zucchero,
cotone e indaco a partire dal tardo settecento. Recentemente sono venuti ad
aggiungere una nuova dimensione alla popolazione sia cittadini di Trinidad
(principalmente rivenditori, dettaglianti, lavoratori ospedalieri e commercianti di
origine indiana) che espatriati, attirati dallo stile di vita rilassato dell'isola.

Da un punto vista culturale tuttavia le radici di Tobago sono rigorosamente afro-
caraibiche, a differenza della diversità cosmopolita di Trinidad. Nelle comunità
montane, il folklore e le credenze africane fioriscono ancora all'ombra delle
ceibe, e nella musica folkloristica il "tambrin" scandisce un ritmo africano. Il
festival annuale di luglio, dedicato al patrimonio storico e culturale, è una
grande esposizione delle migliori tradizioni africane che avviene nei villaggi in
cui si svilupparono, ma in qualsiasi periodo dell'anno è facile imbattersi in una
veglia funebre, una cerimonia di ringraziamento per il raccolto o una "reel
dance" dedicata agli antenati.

Essendo l'industria pesante concentrata a Trinidad, Tobago rimane per la
maggior parte una terra incontaminata. Molti isolani vivono di pesca o
giardinaggio (agricoltura di sussistenza) ma sono sempre più numerosi gli
abitanti che lavorano nel settore del turismo, commercializzando le più preziose
attrazioni dell'isola - le sue magnifiche risorse naturali.

Nel Mar dei Caraibi sudorientale, Tobago è la capitale dell'esplorazione subacquea. Sotto alla superficie del mare si estendono barriere coralline incontaminate, ripide scogliere sottomarine e formazioni vulcaniche che offrono ambienti esaltanti per l'esplorazione subacquea, adatti sia ai principianti che agli esperti. Grazie alla sua fortunatissima posizione, nel punto in cui le acque dell'Orinoco confluiscono con quelle dell'Atlantico e del Mar dei Caraibi, l'isola è circondata da acque ricche di nutrienti e pullulanti di vita: quasi 300 specie di corallo duro; un'ampia varietà di spugne di mare; una miriade di pesci tropicali e di creature del mare più grandi, come balene, squali, delfini, razze molto rare, calamari e tartarughe marine.

Benché la capitale dell'isola sia Scarborough, la capitale dell'esplorazione subacquea è il villaggio di pesca di Speyside. Con la sua diversità di siti e il vortice di correnti di marea attorno alle isole circostanti è un ottimo ambiente per l'immersione in corrente. Benché sia stata creato solo nel 1980, il settore dell'attività subacquea è gestito in modo professionale e secondo le norme internazionali, e Scarborough ha una camera di decompressione gratuita.

In superficie si possono praticare un'infinità di sport: vela Hobie-Cat, kitesurfing e pesca di grosse prede, e chi preferisce un'attività più tranquilla può semplicemente esplorare le barriere coralline sui battelli a chiglia di vetro.

Di ritorno a terra scoprirete che Tobago è stata da molto tempo una mecca per ornitologi, naturalisti ed ecoturisti (compreso David Attenborough, ormai famoso in tutto il mondo, che ha realizzato a Tobago parte della sua serie televisiva intitolata "Trials of Life") ansiosi di scorgere l'emblematico cocrico, fare escursioni attraverso la riserva silvicola, scalare le cascate e osservare le

Charles Scott

tartarughe che si annidano sulla spiaggia di notte. Con le mountain bike inoltre si possono fare ottime escursioni rinvigorenti in alternativa ai viaggi in auto.

Dopo uno stupendo tramonto tropicale, il turista scoprirà una vita notturna del tutto sorprendente che spesso presenta la cultura locale. La festa in spiaggia settimanale Sunday School, organizzata al locale Buccoo, è diventata un appuntamento d'obbligo per abitanti e turisti, come anche le singolari corse di capre e granchi del periodo pasquale e il Tobago Fest, il carnevale di Tobago.

L'economia è alimentata dal turismo e dal settore immobiliare ma l'energia presenta oggi delle autentiche possibilità di diversificazione. Lo sviluppo immobiliare viene attivamente incoraggiato e degli incentivi agli investimenti, come l'esenzione dai dazi doganali sull'importazione di materiali per l'edilizia e di attrezzature turistiche, hanno contribuito a molti dei nuovi complessi edilizi dell'isola, compresi dei grandi centri alberghieri, complessi di ville e due nuovi centri commerciali.

I visitatori ansiosi di investire a Tobago godono non solo di queste esenzioni ma anche della percentuale di concessione immobiliare, che consente loro di possedere fino a due ettari di terreno per scopi commerciali, anche senza essere residenti. Per quanto riguarda la formazione dei lavoratori, il campus di Tobago del Trinidad and Tobago Hospitality and Tourism Training Institute offre corsi di formazione nelle arti artigianali, gastronomia, operazione di viaggi e alberghi e gestione del turismo.

Venite a trascorrere qualche giorno sull'isola e scoprirete perché gli abitanti la chiamano "dolce Tobago".

Tobago: Limpia, verde y serena

LA ISLA CON FORMA de cigarro a la que los amerindios pusieron el nombre de la hoja que les encantaba fumar, la misma que sorprendió tanto a Colón que la llamó "Bellaforma", está situada a 34 kilómetros al nordeste de su isla hermana, Trinidad.

Los 34 kilómetros de largo y 11 de ancho de la tranquila Tobago están rodeados de arrecifes de coral. La baja meseta coralina del sudoeste se eleva gradualmente hasta una cadena central de colinas volcánicas que alcanzan los 630 metros. Por toda la costa Este, las playas de arena blanca, las bahìas aisladas y las ensenadas del Leeward, o la costa caribeña y la ribera rocosa del Atlántico de barlovento, dan paso a un bosque tropical denso (el bosque protegido más antiguo del hemisferio oeste) que cubre las tierras altas atravesadas por valles de rìos y cataratas que fluyen hacia el Sur.

Geológicamente, Tobago ha sido parte del continente sudamericano hasta hace poco. Es por ello que posee una abundancia de flora y fauna, tanto del continente como de la isla, desproporcionada para su tamaño: 210 especies de pájaro, 123 especies de mariposas, 24 tipos de serpientes (todas inofensivas), 17 especies de murciélagos, 16 especies de lagartijas, 14 especies de rana y 12 tipos de mamìferos (incluidos el armadillo, el agouti, el filandro y el pecarì).

Habitada originalmente por amerindios, Tobago se convirtió en un útil peón en el tablero de ajedrez del colonialismo europeo. Colonos provenientes de lo que hoy es Latvia y que se establecieron en 1642, fueron los primeros en llegar. En 1658 fueron expulsados por los holandeses, a quienes siguieron olas sucesivas de invasiones francesas e inglesas hasta que la isla fue cedida a Gran Bretaña

por el Tratado de Parìs de 1802. Tobago se convirtió en una colonia de la Corona Británica en 1877 y tras el hundimiento de la industria del azúcar, se unió a Trinidad como unidad polìtica en 1888.

La mayor parte de la población de 55.000 personas desciende de esclavos africanos transportados hasta aquì para trabajar en las plantaciones de azúcar, algodón e Ìndigo a partir de finales del siglo XVII. En años recientes, los trinitenses locales (principalmente vendedores, tenderos, trabajadores de recibimiento y empresarios provenientes de las Indias Orientales) y los extranjeros residentes, atraìdos por el relajado estilo de vida, han añadido una nueva dimensión a la población.

Sin embargo, culturalmente las raìces de Tobago son estrictamente caribeñas africanas, bien diferentes de la diversidad cosmopolita de Trinidad. El folclore y las creencias africanas aún florecen a la sombra de las ceibas en las comunidades de las laderas de montaña, y al tambor tambrin de la música folk lo marca un ritmo africano. Algunas de las mejores tradiciones africanas se exhiben en sus verdaderos entornos en los pueblos durante el *Heritage Festival* en julio. No obstante, en cualquier época del año se puede uno tropezar con un velatorio, una fiesta de la cosecha o una danza *reel* dedicada a los ancestros.

Como la industria pesada se limita a Trinidad, Tobago permanece mayormente virgen. Muchos isleños se ganan la vida pescando o cultivando (agricultura de subsistencia), pero cada vez son más los que trabajan en el turismo, comercializando el atractivo más valioso de la isla: sus deslumbrantes recursos naturales.

Tobago es el principal destino de buceo en el Sudeste del Caribe. Bajo la

superficie marina, los arrecifes de coral prÌstinos con suaves inclinaciones, los profundos precipicios submarinos y las formaciones volcánicas ofrecen la posibilidad de inmersiones emocionantes, tanto para los principiantes como para los buceadores avanzados. Su ubicación afortunada justo donde coinciden la desembocadura del RÌo Orinoco, el Océano Atlántico y el Mar Caribe, da lugar a unas aguas ricas en nutrientes y abarrotadas de vida: cerca de 300 especies de coral duro; una amplia variedad de esponjas; una mirÌada de peces tropicales y animales marinos de mayor tamaño, como ballenas, tiburones, delfines, rayas poco comunes, calamares y tortugas.

Mientras que Scarborough es la capital nacional de la isla, el pequeño pueblo pesquero de Speyside se ha convertido en la capital del submarinismo, con su diversidad de lugares de inmersión y un vórtice de corrientes con régimen de mareas alrededor de las islas del litoral que garantiza estupendas inmersiones con corrientes. A pesar de haberse establecido tan sólo en los 80, el sector del submarinismo funciona de forma profesional y según los estándares de seguridad internacionales, y Scarborough cuenta con una cámara de descompresión gratuita.

Cualquier deporte de agua concebible se puede practicar, desde la navegación en *Hobie-Cat* hasta el *kitesurfing* y la pesca deportiva. Quienes prefieran un ritmo más pausado apreciarán poder ver los arrecifes desde barcos con fondo de cristal.

Pero volvamos a tierra. Tobago es desde hace mucho tiempo una atracción para ornitólogos, naturalistas y ecoturistas (incluido el internacionalmente reconocido David Attenborough, quien filmó parte de su serie de televisión *Trials of Life* en Tobago) deseosos de ver al emblemático cocrico, hacer senderismo por la Reserva Forestal, escalar cataratas o ver tortugas anidando en la playa por la

Charles Scott

noche. La bicicleta de montaña es una alternativa excelente y vigorizante al recorrido turìstico en coche.

Tras una exquisita puesta de sol tropical, los visitantes descubrirán una vida nocturna sorprendentemente rica y con frecuentes muestras de la cultura local. La fiesta playera semanal de *Sunday School* en Buccoo ya es una institución para locales y visitantes, al igual que las singulares carreras de cabras y cangrejos en Pascua y el carnaval de Tobago: *Tobago Fest*.

La economìa se rige por el turismo y la propiedad inmobiliaria, y ahora se empieza a considerar la energìa como una posibilidad de diversificación real. El desarrollo inmobiliario se promociona activamente, y los incentivos a la inversión, como la desgravación de impuestos aduaneros sobre materiales de construcción importados y equipamiento relacionado con el turismo, han contribuido a la creación de numerosos complejos en la isla, incluidos grandes complejos hoteleros, urbanizaciones de chalés y dos nuevos centros comerciales.

Los visitantes que busquen invertir en Tobago se beneficiarán no sólo de estas desgravaciones, sino también del cupo inmobiliario, que les permite poseer hasta cinco acres de tierra con fines comerciales, incluso sin tener estatus de residentes. En lo referente al desarrollo de la población activa, el recinto universitario del *Hospitality and Tourism Training Institute* de Trinidad y Tobago proporciona formación en artesanado, cocina, hostelerìa y en tour operación y gestión turìstica.

Simplemente pase algún tiempo aquì y descubra por qué los isleños dicen: "Dulce Tobago".

The International dialling code for Trinidad and Tobago is 868

/ Tourist Information Offices

Piarco International Airport, Trinidad. Tel: 669 5196; Crown Point International Airport. Tel: 639 0509; Scarborough Airport. Tel: 639 4333

/ Airport Information Offices

Piarco International Airport, Trinidad. Tel: 669 4868, ext. 4114

Crown Point International Airport. Tel: 639 8547

/ Tobago Department of Tourism

Tobago House of Assembly, 197 Doretta's Court, Mt Marie, Scarborough

Tel: 639 2125. Email: tourbago@tstt.net.tt; www.visittobago.gov.tt

/ Tourism and Industrial Development Company (TIDCO)

Level 1 Maritime Center, 29 Tenth Avenue, Barataria, Trinidad.

Tel: 675 7034; Fax: 638 3560; Email: tourism-info@tidco.tt; www.tidco.co.tt

/ SOS Tobago (Save Our Sea Turtles)

PO Box 27, Scarborough. Tel: 639 0026/9669

Email: info@sos-tobago.org

/ Tobago News

Sangsters Hill, Scarborough. Tel: 660 7107; Fax: 639 5565

Email: ccngroupc@tstt.net.tt

T&T TOURIST OFFICES ABROAD

/ UK

MKI, Mitre Houses, Abbey Road, Bush Hill Park,

Enfield, Middlesex EN1 2QE

Tel: (020) 8350 1009; Fax: (020) 8350 1011

Email: mki@ttg.co.uk; www.mki.ltd.uk

/ USA

Keating Communications, 350 Fifth Avenue, New York, NY 10118 USA

Tel: (212) 760 2400; Fax: (212) 760 6402

Cheryl Andrews Marketing Inc, 1500 San Remo, Suite 145, Coral Gables, Florida 33146. Tel: 1 305 663 1660; Fax: 1 305 666 9728

/ Canada

512 Duplex Avenue, Toronto, Ontario M4R 2E3

Tel: (416) 485 7827; Fax: (416) 485 8256

Email: assoc@thermgroup.ca; www.visittnt.com

Arnos Vale Hotel

Blue Waters Inn

Coco Reef Resort and Spa

/ **Adventure Eco Villas**

Arnos Vale Road, Plymouth. Tel: 639 2839; Fax: 639 4197
Email: adventure@tstt.net.tt; www.adventure-ecovillas.com

/ **Arnos Vale Hotel**

The Arnos Vale Estate, Plymouth. Tel: 639 2881/2, 660-0815; Fax: 639 4629
Email: reservations@arnosvalehotel.com; www.arnosvalehotel.com

/ **Arthur's by the Sea**

Crown Point. Tel: 639 0196; Fax: 639 0196
Email: arthurs@trinidad.net; www.trinidad.net/arthurs

/ **Belleviste Apartments**

PO Box, 69, Scarborough. Tel: 639 2631; Fax: 639 3691
Email: almandoz@tstt.net.tt; www.trinidad.net/belleviste

/ **Bijou des Caraibes**

3 Jacamar Drive, Mt Irvine. Tel:639 9604; Fax: 639 0501
Email: gemjud@tstt.net.tt; www.bijou-des-caraibes.com

/ **Blue Haven Hotel**

c/o Robinson Crusoe Beach Resort Ltd, Bacolet Bay, Scarborough.
Tel: 660 7400, 660 7500, 660 7600; Fax: 660 7900
Email: reservations@bluehavenhotel.com; www.bluehavenhotel.com

/ **Blue Horizon Resort**

Jacamar Drive, Mt Irvine. Tel: 639 0433; Fax: 639 0432; www.blue-horizonresort.com

/ **Blue Mango Cottages**

Bay Road, Castara. Tel: 639 2060; Fax: 639 5414
Email: bluemang@tstt.net.tt; www.blue-mango.com

/ **Blue Waters Inn**

Batteaux Bay, Speyside. Tel: 660 4341, 660 4077, 660 2583; Fax: 660 5195
Email: bwi@bluewatersinn.com; www.bluewatersinn.com

/ **Canoe Bay Beach Resort**

Cove Estate, Lowlands. Tel: 639 0540, 685 4785; 678 5839, 631 0367
Fax: 639-0540; Email: canoebay@find-us.net; www.find-us.net/canoebay,
www.simplytobago.com, www.mytobago.com

/ **Coco Reef Resort and Spa**

Coconut Bay, PO Box 434, Scarborough. Tel: 639 8572; Fax: 639 8574
Email: cocoreef-tobago@trinidad.net; www.cocoreef.com

Conrado Beach Resort

Footprints Eco Resort

Grafton Beach Resort

Hilton Tobago Golf & Spa Resort

/ **Cocrico Inn & Courlan Bay Villas**

North and Commissioner Streets, Plymouth. Tel: 639 2961; Fax: 639 6565

Email: cocrico@tstt.net.tt; www.hews-tours.com/cocricoinn

/ **Conrado Beach Resort**

PO Box 405, Scarborough. Tel: 639 0145; Fax: 639 0755; Email: conrado@tstt.net.tt

/ **Coral Reef Guest House**

Lowlands. Tel: 639 2536; Fax: 639 0070; Email: Richard@smsworldplus.com

/ **Crown Point Hotel**

Crown Point. Tel: 639 8781; Fax: 639 8731

Email: crownpoint@sunsurfsand.com; www.crownpoint beachhotel.com

/ **Cuffie River Nature Retreat**

Runnemede Local Road, Runnemede. Tel: 660 0505; Fax: 660 0606

Email: cuffiriv@tstt.net.tt; www.cuffie-river.com

/ **Della Mira Guest House** 36 Bacolet Street, Scarborough. Tel: 639 2531

/ **Footprints Eco Resort**

Culloden Bay Road, via Golden Lane. Tel: 660 0118; Fax: 660 0027

Email: footprints@trinidad.net, kpamora@trinidad.net;

www.footprintseco-resort.com

/ **Golden Thistle Hotel** Store Bay. Fax: 639 8521; Email: Clyde@trinidad.net

/ **Grafton Beach Resort**

Black Rock. Tel: 639 0191; Fax: 639 0030

Email: grafton@singhs.com; www.grafton-resort.com

/ **Hilton Tobago Golf & Spa Resort**

Lowlands, Scarborough. Tel: 660 8500; Fax: 660 8503

Email: tobhilt@tstt.net.tt; www.hilton.com

/ **Jammev Beach Resort**

Tobago Plantations, Villa 91, Lowlands Estate. Tel: 623 0143; Fax: 623 0143

Email: xtatik@tstt.net.tt; www.xtatik.com

/ **Jimmy's Holiday Resort**

Milford Road, Crown Point. Tel: 639 8292, 639 8929; Fax: 639 3100

Email: jimmys@tstt.net.tt

Kariwak Village Hotel

Le Grand Courlan Resort

/ Kariwak Village Hotel

Store Bay Local Road, Crown Point. Tel: 639 8442; Fax: 639 8441

Email: kariwak@tstt.net.tt; www.kariwak.com

/ Le Grand Courlan Resort and Spa

Black Rock. Tel: 639 9667; Fax: 639 9292

Email: legrand@singhs.com; www.legrandcourlan-resort.com

/ Man-O-War Bay Cottages

Charlotteville. Tel: 660 4327; Fax: 660 4328

www.man-o-warbaycottages.com, www.villastobago.com

/ Manta Lodge Speyside. Tel: 660 5268

/ Mt Irvine Bay Hotel & Golf Club Mt Irvine. Tel: 639 8872

/ The Palms Villa Resort

Signal Hill Old Road, Signal Hill. Tel: 635 1010; Fax: 635 1011

Email: info@thepalmstobago.com; www.thepalmstobago.com

/ Plantation Beach Villas

Stonehaven, Black Rock. Tel: 639 9377; Fax: 639 0455

Email: villas@wow.net; www.plantationbeachvillas.com

/ Richmond Great House Inn Belle Garden. Tel: 660 4467; Fax: 660 4467

/ Sandy Point Crown Point. Tel: 629 8533

/ Sameeha Gardens Carnbee #1, Carnbee. Tel: 660 8000; Fax: 631 8080

/ SeaShells Villas

Bon Accord Estate, Bon Accord. Tel: 639 9600; Fax: 639 4433

Email: villas@tstt.net.tt; www.seashellsvillas.com

/ Speyside Inn

Speyside. Tel: 660 4852; Email: speysideinn@trinidad.net

/ Sundeck Apartments

Main Road, Castara. Tel: 639 1410; Fax: 635 2252

Email: sundeck@tstt.net.tt; www.sundeckapartments.com

/ Surfside Hotel

Crown Point. Tel: 639 2418; Fax: 639 0614; Email: surfside@tstt.net.tt

Villa Being

/ **Tobago Villas on the Green**
Jacamar Drive, Mt Irvine. Tel: 632 4608; Fax: 632 4608
Email: enquiries@tobagovillasonthegreen.com
www.tobagovillasonthegreen.com

/ **Top Ranking Hill View Guesthouse**
Speyside. Tel: 660 4904; Fax: 660 4904
Email: toprank00@yahoo.com; www.caribinfo.com

/ **Tropikist Beach Hotel and Resort**
Crown Point. Tel: 639 8512, 639 8513; Fax: 639 9605
Email: tropikist@wow.net; www.tropikist.com

/ **The Caribbean's Premier Nature Resort**
Woodlands. Tel: 639 6816; Fax: 639 6841
Email: info@imortelle.com; www.imortelle.com

/ **The Villas at Stonehaven**
PO Box 1079, Bon Accord, Black Rock. Tel: 639 0361; Fax: 639 0102
Email: stonehav@tstt.net.tt; www.stonehavenvillas.com

/ **Toucan Inn** Crown Point. Tel: 629 7173; Fax: 639 8933

/ **Tropikist Beach Hotel**
Crown Point. Tel: 639 8512; Fax: 639 9605
Email: tropikist@wow.net; www.tropikist.com

/ **Turtle Beach Hotel** Courlan Bay, Plymouth. Tel: 639 2636

/ **Villa Being**
Arnos Vale. Tel: 625 4443; Fax: 625 4420
Email: info@being-thevillaexperience.com; www.being-villaexperience.com

/ **Villa Sans Souci**
Villa 84, Tobago Plantations, Lowlands. Tel: 628 3334; Fax: 622 3232
Email: info@villa-sans-souci.com; www.villa-sans-souci.com

/ **Viola's Place**
101 Hamden Road, Lowlands. Tel: 639 9441; Fax: 639 9441
Email: violas@tstt.net.tt; www.violasplace.com

/ **Wood's Castle Holiday Resort**
Crown Point. Tel: 639 0803

/ Arnos Vale Hotel

The Arnos Vale Estate, Plymouth. Tel: 639 2881/2, 660 0815; Fax: 639 4629

Email: reservations@arnosvalehotel.com; www.arnosvalehotel.com

Cuisine: *New World/Creole*

/ Café Iguana

Corner Store Bay Local Road, Crown Point. Tel: 631 8205; Fax: 631 8205

Email: iguana@trinidad.net; www.cafeiguana.com

Cuisine: *International/Caribbean/Cocktails*

/ Café Coco Restaurant

First Left off Pigeon Point Road, Crown Point. Tel: 639 0996; Fax: 639 8574

Email: cocoreef-tobago@trinidad.net; wwwcocoreef.com

Cuisine: *International/Caribbean*

/ Café Mélange & The Caribbean Chulha Restaurant

133 Shirvan Road (opposite Island Investments). Tel: 631 0121; Fax: 631 1260

Cuisine: *Fusion Creole*

Arnos Vale Hotel Restaurant

/ Coral Reef Restaurant

Hilton Tobago, Lowlands, Scarborough. Tel: 660 8500; Fax: 660 8503

Email: tobhilt@tstt.net.tt; www.hilton.com

Cuisine: *Seafood/International*

/ Diver's Den Grill

7 Robert Street, Bon Accord. Tel: 639 0287; Fax: 660 7264

Email: info@diversdentobago.com; www.diversdentobago.com

Cuisine: *Local and International grilled foods*

/ Kariwak Village Restaurant

Store Bay Local Road, Crown Point.

Tel: 639 8442; Fax: 639 8441; Email: kariwak@tstt.net.tt; www.kariwak.com

Cuisine: *Caribbean/Creole/International*

Kariwak Village Restaurant

/ La Tartaruga Italian Restaurant

Buccoo Bay Main Road, opposite Buccoo Beach. Tel: 639 0940; Fax: 639 5482

Email: info@latartarugatobago.com; www.latartarugatobago.com

Cuisine: *Italian*

/ La Terrazza

Shirvan Road, Buccoo. Tel: 639 8242; Fax: 639 8242

Email: tavacocigars@hotmail.com

Cuisine: *Italian*

/ Meshell's

Corner Shirvan and Buccoo Roads. Tel: 631 0353, 682 3334

Email: meshellsoftobago@hotmail.com

Cuisine: *International/Caribbean*

/ Patino's Restaurant and Bar

Shirvan Road, Buccoo. Tel: 639 9481; Fax: 639 9481

Email: infokpresorts.com, www.kpresorts.com

Cuisine: *International/Seafood/Cocktails*

/ The Pavilion

PO Box 1079, Bon Accord, Black Rock. Tel: 639 0361; Fax: 639 0102

Email: stonehav@tstt.net.tt; www.stonehavenvillas.com

Cuisine: *International/Caribbean*

/ Pelican Reef

Milford Road, Crown Point.

Tel: 660 8000; Fax: 631 8080; Email: jazar@tstt.net.tt

Cuisine: *Seafood/Steaks*

/ Seahorse Inn

Grafton Beach Road, Black Rock. Tel: 639 0686; Fax: 639 0057

Email: seahorse@trinidad.net; www.seahorseinntobago.com

Cuisine: *Seafood and Steaks; Creole/International*

/ Shirvan Watermill Restaurant

Shirvan Road, Mount Pleasant. Tel: 639 0000; Fax: 639 0534

Email: swmill@tstt.net.tt

Cuisine: *Creole/International/Seafood*

A view over Grafton Beach Resort in Black Rock, base for Singh's Auto Rentals

/ Auto Rentals (Tobago)
Crown Point International Airport. Tel: 639 0644, 639 0305; Fax: 639 0305

/ Baird's Rentals Ltd
Crown Point International Airport. Tel: 639 7054,
Scarborough, Tel: 639 2528, 684 0979, 681 8225, Fax: 639 4126
Email: baird_griffith@hotmail.com

/ Econo Car Rentals (Tobago)
Local Road (opposite Crown Point International Airport).
Tel: 660 8728
Email: econo_car@hotmail.com; www.trinidad.net/econocar

/ Hillcrest Car Rental Services Ltd
47 Mt Pelier Trace, Scarborough.
Tel: 660 8361 (Crown Point), 639 5208 (Scarborough); Fax: 639 5208
Email: hcrest@tstt.net.tt; www.hcrestcar.com

/ Sherman's Auto Rentals
Lambeau Village. Tel: 639 2292; Fax: 639 3084
Email: shermans@trinidad.net; www.shermansrental.com

/ Singh's Auto Rentals Ltd
c/o Grafton Beach Resort, Black Rock.
Tel: 639 0191; Fax: 639 0030

/ Thrifty/Rodriguez Car Rental Ltd
Crown Point International Airport. Tel: 639 8507, 639 8062 (6am-9pm)
Turtle Beach Hotel; Tel: 639 8111 (8am-11am), 639 8507; Fax: 639 0357
Email: eontab@tstt.net.tt; www.thrifty.com

/ Classic Tours Tobago Ltd

Crown Point International Airport. Tel: 639 9891; Fax: 639 9892

Email: info@classictoursltd.com; www.classictoursltd.com

An innovative destination management company, offering a full range of services to visitors and locals of both islands.

/ Frankie Tours and Rentals

Easterfield Road, Mason Hall. Tel: 639 4527, 681 3717

Email: frankgem@tstt.net.tt; www.frankietourstobago.com

Island tours, rain forest, fishing, nightclubs, barbecues, reefs, bird watching, car rentals, and taxi services.

/ Yes Tourism

Surfside Hotel, Pigeon Point Road, Crown Point. Tel: 631 0286; Fax: 631 0287

Email: info@yes-tourism.com; www.yes-tourism.com

/ Information about Eco Holidays and tours in Tobago

Pat Turpin, Pioneer Journeys, Man-O-War Bay, Cottages, Charlotteville. Tel: 660 4327

David Rooks, Nature Tours, PO Box 348, Scarborough. Tel: 639 4276; Email: rookstobago@trinidad.net

Margaret Hinkson, Educatours, Carnbee. Tel: 639 7422

For information on other tour services, or a list of trained birders and approved tour guides, contact the THA's Department of Tourism. Tel: 639 0509

Blue Waters Inn

/ Adventure Eco Divers
PO Box 1102, Canaan. Tel: 639 8729; Fax: 639 3993
Email: ecodiver@tstt.net.tt; www.adventuredivers.com
Member of Divers Alert Network (DAN).

/ Cocomotion
PO Box 1100, Bon Accord. Tel: 686 0082; Fax: 639 2449
Email: cocomo@tstt.net.tt; www.cocomotion.net

/ Extra Divers Tobago
Surfside Hotel, Pigeon Point Road. Tel: 639 7424, 686-9622; Fax: 639 7424
Email: extradivers@tstt.net.tt; www.extra_divers.net
PADI and CMAS courses taught in German and English.

/ R and Sea Divers
Spence Trace, Crown Point. Tel: 639 8120; Fax: 639 8120
Email: rsdivers@tstt.net.tt; www.rseadivers.com

/ Scuba Adventure Safari
Pigeon Point Road, Crown Point. Tel: 660 7767, 620-9285; Fax: 660 7333
Email: info@divetobago.com; www.divetobago.com

/ World of Watersports
Lowlands Estate, PO Box 299. Tel: 660 7234; Fax: 660 8326

Crown Point

/ **Store Bay** - small beach with beautiful clear water, boat and reef trips, beach vendors, finishing line for August's Great Race power boat and venue for Great Fete.

/ **Pigeon Point** - Tobago's celebrity beach. White sand, lagoon protected by Buccoo Reef, palms and almond trees, thatched huts, bar and snacks, boats, watersports and reef trips.

/ **Sandy Point** - relatively quiet, white sand bordered by sea grapes and palms.

/ **Canoe Bay** - an Amerindian site with attractive beach, shallow water, largely unvisited.

Scarborough area

/ **Little Rockly Bay** - long idyllic stretch shaded by coconut trees.
/ **Petit Trou** - long breezy walking beach in Lowlands.
/ **Bacolet Bay** - small secluded black sand, crescent shaped beach. Location for Swiss Family Robinson movie, popular with surfers.
/ **Minster Bay** - around Bacolet Point, also popular with surfers.

Buccoo to Plymouth

/ **Buccoo** - narrow beach on protected bay in delightful fishing village where both Sunday School, Goat and Crab races held at Easter.
/ **Mt Irvine Bay** - long stretch popular with surfers Dec-Mar.
/ **Stonehaven Bay/Grafton Beach** - magnificent sweep of coarse sand, sometimes with powerful waves.
/ **Turtle Beach** - nesting site for Giant Leatherbacks Mar-Aug.
/ **Back Bay** - quiet and secluded.

Leeward Coast

/ **King Peter's Bay** - deserted yellow sand beach.
/ **Castara** - curving stretch of white sand, with couple of restaurants. Mostly quiet but good spot to meet fishermen and villagers.
/ **Englishman's Bay** - hidden from the road, a spectacular deserted beach with pure white sand, deep calm water.
/ **Parlatuvier** - another perfect beach, which shelves steeply and where waves can be strong.
/ **Bloody Bay** - the last beach accessible by road, gloriously golden and empty.
/ **Dead Bay and Cotton Bay** - are highly recommended by locals who you will need as guides, the first only accessible by hiking, the second by boat.

Windward Coast

/ **Pinfold Bay** - next to ruins of Fort Granby.
/ **King's Bay** - One of best beaches, former site of large Carib settlement. On a horseshoe bay with calm water, reefs, dark sand shaded by coconut trees.
/ **Speyside** - sandy beaches within swimming distance of the reefs.
/ **Batteaux Bay** - stunning deep blue water and reefs off secluded shore.
/ **Man O'War Bay** - Charlotteville's beautiful sandy beach, ideal for swimming.

Le Grand Courlan Resort

New laws have made it easy and convenient to get married in Tobago. Three days' local residence and a minor amount of paperwork, is all it takes. Many hotels are happy to help you with wedding arrangements, catering and providing accommodation for guests. They will take care of the paperwork and arrange special extras such as a priest or minister, a steel band or a videotape of the ceremony. The more imaginative (or adventurous) can be married on a beach, a boat, under a waterfall or even 40 feet underwater.

Whatever your choice, it's just a Special Marriage Licence away. Once you have been in the country three days, you can apply for one at the Warden's Office IDC Mall. The licence costs TT$30; valid identification (passport) is required and widow(er)s or divorced persons must show documentary proof. For a further fee of TT$50, the ceremony can be performed in the Warden's Office. The marriage certificate must subsequently be taken to the Registry Office in Scarborough to be registered. Stamp duty for this service is TT$25

Blue Waters Inn

Tobago Tourism Authority

Watersports

/ **Windsurfing:** Pigeon Point, Mt Irvine, Black Rock, Speyside, Minister Bay
/ **Waterskiing, step-jets, hobie-cats, sailboats, kayaks, catamarans:** Pigeon Point, Mt Irvine, Black Rock, Speyside
/ **Snorkelling:** Store Bay, Pigeon Pt/Buccoo Reef, Mt Irvine, Speyside
/ **Scuba diving:** Buccoo Reef, Mt Irvine, Arnos Vale, Culloden Bay, Speyside, Charlotteville
/ **Dive shops** are located at Arnos Vale, Black Rock, Culloden Bay, Charlotteville, Pigeon Point, Speyside, and Store Bay.

Deep sea fishing

Barracuda Charters, Petit Valley Diego Martin TT, 637 0134
Bayshore Charters, Petit Valley Trinidad, 680 4426
Blue Magic Charters Ltd, Scarborough Trinidad & Tobago, 639 3212
Dream Catcher Marine Charters, Grafton Tobago, 680 7457
Excellent Charters, Port Of Spain Trinidad, (809) 623 6464
Hard Play Sport Fishing Charters, Canaan Tobago, 639 7108
Mount Irvine Watersports, Bon Accord Tobago, 639 9379
TNT Charters Ltd, Port of Spain Trinidad, 632 3974
Mt Irvine Watersports, 639 9379
Grafton Beach Resort, 639 0191
Le Gran Courlan Resort, 639 9667
Kalina Cats, 639 6306
Blue Waters Inn, 660 2583
Dillons Deep Sea Charters, 639 8765

Blue Waters Inn

Hilton Tobago Golf & Spa Resort

Aqua-aerobics

Le Grand Courlan, 639 9667; **Golf Mt Irvine**, 639 8871;
Tobago Plantations, 639 8000

Horseback riding

Friendship Riding Stables, 660 8563

Mountain biking

Slowleaktours, 635 0641/681 5695;
www.outdoor-tobago.com/mountainbike/guide.html.
Mountain Biking Tobago, 639 9709; Email: mtbtobago@tstt.net.tt

Squash

Grafton Beach Resort, 639 0191

Table tennis

Rex Turtle Beach Hotel, 639 2851

Tennis

Arnos Vale Hotel, 639 2881/2, **Blue Waters Inn**, 660 2583;
Le Grand Courlan, 639 9667; **Store Bay** and **Turtle Beach Hotel**

Golf

Mt Irvine, 639 8871; **Tobago Plantations Lowlands Estate Golf and
Country Club**, 639 8000; **Hilton Tobago Golf & Spa Resort**
Lowlands 660 8500

Waterpolo

Hilton Tobago, 660 8500

Yoga

Hilton Tobago, 660 8500

The International dialling code for Trinidad and Tobago is 868